TV Times

ALL STAR COOKERY

ALL STAR COOKERY

JILL COX

First published in 1988 by Boxtree Limited.
Published in association with
Independent Television Books Ltd.

Text Copyright © Jill Cox 1988

Designed by Groom and Pickerill
Typeset by York House Typographic
Printed in Italy
for Boxtree Limited,
36 Tavistock Street,
London WC2E 7PB

British Library Cataloguing in Publication Data

Cox, Jill
   All star cookery
   1. Food – Recipes
   I. Title
   641.5

   ISBN 1-85283-238-X

Contents

Introduction

Although most of us are familiar with the screen image of TV celebrities, it's always fascinating to learn a little about their private lives. And probably the most riveting information is about how they cook and what they eat. Each week in *TVTimes*, a famous TV star talks about his or her likes and dislikes, shares cookery ideas and recipes, and often shows us round the kitchen, too. As with any other profession, TV stars differ in their preferences, and this book is a varied collection of recipes from the tables of your favourite entertainers.

For the main part, *All Star Cookery* is divided into recipe sections with soups, starters, main courses, puddings and cakes, cookery for children and for Christmas, packed with dishes enjoyed by the stars. But quite often, a celebrity gives such an unusual interview to *TVTimes*, it makes a fascinating story in itself. So in between the recipe pages, there are special sections on, for example, Italian food, much loved by both *Michael Aspel* and *Kate Robbins*, Indian food from *Mike Morris*, fish barbecues from *Oliver Tobias*, and fondues from *David Jensen*.

It was interesting to find out that *Maureen Lipman* loves serving Scandinavian food, partly because over the years she has had Swedish and Norwegian au pairs living in the family home. Or to learn how *Bobby Davro* lost weight with his delicious low-fat recipes.

If you're planning an all-star dinner party, choose dishes which complement each other both in texture and colour. Avoid, for example, food which is all pale, or all creamy. It won't look appetising, however good it tastes. And it's quite a good idea to plan on at least one cold course. A cold first course, for example, can be made in advance and chilled, which leaves more time to put the finishing touches to a hot main course – and entertain guests at the same time. Summer dinners are best ended with fresh fruit or something light, dainty and chilled. Although in the winter, few would turn down traditional English pud like treacle tart or jam roly poly, much loved by many TV stars, especially *Lionel Blair*.

Choosing wine is something most celebrities have definite ideas about. But like the rest of us, many shop in supermarkets and High Street off-licences for their wine where excellent value-for-money bargains are always available. There is no wine which is the only one you should serve with a particular recipe. Some combinations work better than others, but this is usually a matter of logic combined with personal taste. It is sensible not to serve an expensive wine with a searing hot curry, for example – you simply wouldn't be able to taste it. But if in doubt most supermarkets give recommendations on the label, and your local off-licencee should be only too happy to advise. Nevertheless, if you like white wine with everything – nobody is to say you're wrong.

As well as recipes for entertaining, this book is packed with everyday dishes that are quick, economical and easy to make. TV stars, like most other people, are busy working, or looking after their families, or both. So budget meals and family dinners are part of their regular routines, too. It's good to know that in spite of the glamour of their profession, they're really just like you or me!

Cooking Charts

Quantities in this book are given in both imperial and metric. They are not exact conversions as 1 oz is actually the equivalent of 28 grams – not a convenient figure to work with. So generally the measures have been converted to 1 oz equal to 25 grams for simplification. But since *some* recipes are converted on a proportional basis only use one set of measurements. Don't try to mix them. This applies to the conversion of fluids from imperial to metric, too. The tables below and opposite give an *approximate* conversion of imperial to metric measurements. Although these can be used as a general reference, you should always follow the figures given for the recipe you are making.

Ounces	Grams
1	25
2	50
3	75
4	100
5	150
6	175
7	200
8/½lb	225
9	250
10	275
11	300
12	350
13	375
14	400
15	425
16/1lb	450
17	475
18	500
19	550
20/1¼lbs	575

Fl oz	Pints	Mls
1		25
2		50
3		75
4		100
5	¼	150
6		175
7		200
8		225
9		250
10	½	300
11		325
12		350
13		375
14		400
15	¾	425
16		450
17		475
18		500
19		550
20	1 pint	600
30	1½	825
35	1¾	1000

Oven temperatures

	Gas	°F	°C
Very cool	¼	225	110
	½	250	120
Cool	1	275	140
	2	300	150
Moderate	3	325	160
	4	350	180
Hottish	5	375	190
	6	400	200
Hot	7	425	220
	8	450	230
Very hot	9	475	240
	10	500	260

Soups and Starters

First courses should be delicate appetisers designed to alert the taste-buds for the meal to come. The best starters perk up the appetite and look as good as they taste.
Soup can be a warming or a cooling start to a meal. Some are substantial and a meal in themselves, whilst others are light and delicate.

STRIKER'S SOUP

At half time during his sporting commentaries, *Brian Moore* goes for a warming vegetable soup.

1 onion, peeled and chopped
2 carrots, peeled and diced
2 sticks celery, chopped
1 potato, peeled and diced
1 parsnip, peeled and diced
2 leeks, trimmed and sliced
2 courgettes, chopped
1 oz/25 g butter
1½ pints/850 ml chicken stock
salt, pepper, bay leaf

Fry vegetables gently in butter for 5 minutes. Add stock, salt and pepper and bay leaf. Simmer for 15 minutes.

Serves 6

APRICOT SOUP

Christmas first-course in Austria is often a refreshing fruit soup, delicately flavoured and unusual, says *Anneka Rice*.

2 × 15 oz/425 ml tins apricots, drained
½ pint/300 ml dry white wine
½ tsp nutmeg
3 tbsp double cream

Purée apricots. Stir in wine, nutmeg and cream. Chill and pour into soup bowls.

Serves 4

CULLEN SKINK NESSIE

Scottish actress *Siobhan Redman's* Auntie Nessie spoils her with this traditional smoked haddock and potato soup.

8 oz/225 g haddock fillet
1¾ pt/1 litre water
1 medium onion, sliced
salt and pepper
½ pt/300 ml milk
1 lb/450 g mashed potatoes
1 tbsp fresh chopped parsley
4 tbsp single cream

Place fish in water with onion and seasoning. Cover and simmer for 20 minutes. Remove fish, skin it, then flake flesh. Stir potatoes into liquid; add fish and milk. Reheat, and check seasoning. Garnish each serving with parsley and a tablespoon of cream.

Serves 4

BLARNEY BROTH

A potato addict, Irish *Roy Walker* likes this filling and nourishing leek and potato soup.

1 large onion, peeled and sliced
2 leeks, trimmed and sliced
2 oz/50 g butter
1 lb/450 g potatoes, peeled and diced
1½ pints/850 ml chicken stock
salt and pepper
pinch ground mace
4 tbsp single cream

Irish comic Roy Walker toasts St. Patrick's day with a traditional glass of Guiness. Potato dishes are on pages 61-62.

Fry onion and leeks in butter until soft. Add potatoes, chicken stock, mace and seasoning. Bring to boil and simmer 15-20 minutes. Pour into blender and purée until smooth. Stir in cream and reheat without boiling.

Serves 4

SCOOP

A curried vegetable soup from *Derek Jameson*.

1 oz/25 g butter
1 large onion, peeled and chopped
8 oz/225 g potatoes, peeled and chopped
7 oz/200 g tin tomatoes
½ pint/300 ml beef stock
dash of Worcestershire sauce
1 tsp curry powder
1 oz/25 g cooked long grain rice
salt and freshly ground black pepper

Melt butter in a large pan and add onion. Cook until soft. Stir in potatoes and cook over a low heat for 20 minutes. Add tomatoes then blend until smooth. Return to pan, add stock, Worcestershire sauce, curry powder, rice, salt and pepper and reheat to serve.

Serves 4

ROOTY

A spicy parsnip soup which actor *Rory McGrath* says is substantial and satisfying.

1 onion, peeled and chopped
1 clove garlic, crushed
1 oz/25 g butter
1 tbsp oil
1 tsp ground coriander
1 tsp chilli powder
2 lb/900 g parsnips, peeled and diced
1½ pints/850 ml chicken stock
1 bay leaf
salt and pepper
¼ pint/150 ml single cream

Fry onion and garlic in butter and oil until soft. Add coriander, chilli and parsnips and cook for 5 minutes, stirring all the time. Pour over stock, add bay leaf, season with salt and pepper. Bring to boil and simmer for 20 minutes. Blend until smooth, stir in cream and reheat before serving.

Serves 4

LIGHTNING PARSNIP SOUP

Denis Norden cooked up this mild, spiced parsnip soup the day he boiled a pan of parsnips to a mush.

1 onion, peeled and chopped
2 tbsp oil
6 rashers streaky bacon, chopped
2 tsp curry powder
salt and pepper
1 bay leaf
1 pint/600 ml chicken stock
1 lb overcooked parsnips
¼ pint/150 ml single cream

Fry onion in oil until soft. Add bacon and fry until cooked. Reserve a tbsp for garnish. Stir in curry powder, salt and pepper, bay leaf, and cook for 1 minute. Stir in stock. Add parsnips and bring to boil. Simmer for few minutes then blend until smooth. Stir in cream, season and reheat. Garnish with reserved bacon.

Serves 4-6

FRENCH ONION SOUP

Traditional French winter warmer from *Prunella Scales*.

4 large onions, peeled and cut into rings
2 tbsp oil
1 tbsp soft brown sugar
2 pints/1.2 litre beef stock
1 bay leaf
salt and fresh ground black pepper
1 small French bread stick, cut into slices
2 oz/50 g Gruyère cheese, grated

Place onions and oil in a pan, cover and cook for 15 minutes over low heat. Stir in sugar and increase heat until browned. Stir in stock, add bay leaf and seasoning, then bring to boil. Simmer for 10 minutes. Toast bread on one side, sprinkle grated cheese on other side and grill until bubbling. Remove bay leaf and pour soup into warmed bowls. Place toasted bread on top.

Serves 6

MARSUPIAL SOUP

Housewife and superstar *Dame Edna Everage* usually bases this on a stock of choice bandicoot segments, wallaby shanks, paunch of koala and a variety of giblets. But you can use the more readily obtainable chicken stock.

1 onion, peeled and chopped
1 stick celery, chopped
1 tbsp oil
1 lb/450 g broccoli, washed and roughly chopped
1 bunch of watercress, washed
1½ pints/850 ml chicken stock
salt and black pepper
½ tsp nutmeg
watercress, to garnish

Cook onion and celery in oil until soft in a large pan. Add broccoli, watercress, stock, seasoning and nutmeg, and simmer for 12 minutes. Remove, and blend until smooth. Serve garnished with watercress.

Serves 4

PARSLEY SOUP

A rampant parsley bed was the reason *Penelope Keith* invented this deep green, fragrant and tasty soup.

1 oz/25 g butter
1 medium onion, chopped
1 clove garlic, chopped
8 oz/225 g parsley, roughly chopped
½ level tbsp plain flour
1 pint/600 ml chicken stock
salt and fresh ground white pepper
¼ pint/150 ml double cream
fresh chopped parsley for garnish

Melt butter and cook the onion and garlic slowly for 3-4 minutes. Stir in the parsley, then scatter on the flour. Stir and cook for one minute more, then gradually add the stock. Bring to the boil, then reduce heat to simmer. Purée in a blender. Season and add cream. Reheat without boiling. Serve in warmed bowls.

Serves 2

SOUP SOLITAIRE

Spicy carrot soup topped with a swirl of cream which actress *Susie Blake* recommends for a filling snack.

½ small onion, peeled and chopped
1 small potato, peeled and diced
6 oz/175 g carrots, peeled and chopped
1 tbsp oil
large pinch each of chilli, turmeric, ground coriander and cumin
½ pint/300 ml chicken stock
salt and fresh ground black pepper
1 tbsp double cream

Fry onion, potato and carrot in oil for 5 minutes. Stir in spices and stock. Bring to boil, cover and simmer for 12 minutes, stirring occasionally until carrot and potato are tender. Blend until smooth. Return to pan, season and reheat. Pour into a warmed bowl and add a swirl of cream.

Serves 1

SALMON AND POTATO SOUP

This delicious, white, creamy soup of salmon and potato pieces was discovered by the cycling chef, *Tom Vernon*, on his travels in Finland.

1 onion, peeled and chopped
1 oz/25 g butter
4 potatoes, peeled, parboiled and chopped
1½ pints/850 ml fish stock
1 lb/450 g salmon fillet, cut into chunks
2 tbsp dill, chopped
salt and pepper
¼ pint/150 ml single cream

Fry onion in butter until soft. Add pototoes, stock, salmon and bring to the boil. Simmer for 5 minutes, then add dill, salt, pepper and cream. Reheat gently before serving.

Serves 4

Pictured above is 'Fatman' Tom Vernon preparing a delicious dish from his worldwide travels.

Actress Penelope Keith ladling a bowl of fresh-tasting Parsley Soup (see page 10).

IN THE POT

A good idea from *Richard Briers* for making the most of a chicken carcase for a tasty stock.

Stock
1 cooked chicken carcase
2 pints/1.2 litre water
1 bouquet garni
1 carrot, peeled
1 onion, peeled
salt and pepper

1 onion, peeled and chopped
1 parsnip, peeled and diced
2 carrots, peeled and diced
4 sticks celery, chopped
1 oz/25 g butter

For stock, put chicken carcase in large pot. Cover with water. Add bouquet garni, carrot and onion. Season. Bring to boil. Simmer for one hour. Skim surface. Strain stock into jug to give 1½ pints/ 850 ml. Remove chicken meat from carcase. Put to one side. Discard bones.

Fry onion, parsnip, carrots and celery in butter for 5 minutes. Add stock. Bring to boil. Gently simmer for 15 minutes. Cut chicken into strips. Add to soup. Reheat and serve.

Serves 4

These two delicious first courses were dreamed up by *Ray Brook*'s local pub by the river at Kew Bridge. AVOCADO BAKE is an exotic and rather surprising way of serving avocado. In DEEP-FRIED BRIE golden cubes of Brie are cooked to oozing perfection.

AVOCADO BAKE

½ pint/300 ml milk
1 onion, peeled and stuck with cloves
1 small carrot, peeled
1 bouquet garni
1 oz/25 g butter
1 oz/25 g flour
salt and pepper
7 oz/200 g tin tuna, drained and flaked
2 avocado pears, halved and stoned
4 oz/100 g Cheddar cheese, grated
paprika pepper

Pour milk over onion, carrot and bouquet garni in a pan. Bring to boil, then remove from heat. Infuse for 30 minutes to allow milk to take on flavour of vegetables and herbs. Strain milk.

Melt butter in a pan, stir in flour and cook for 2 minutes. Remove from heat, gradually stir in milk, then return to heat. Bring to boil and simmer for 3-4 minutes until thick. Season, and stir in tuna.

Spoon sauce generously over avocado halves. Place on baking tray, sprinkle with cheese and paprika. Bake at Gas 6/400°F/200°C for 15 minutes or until cheese begins to bubble.

Serves 4

DEEP-FRIED BRIE

1 lb/450 g Brie, chilled
1 egg, beaten
4 oz/100 g white breadcrumbs

Cut Brie into 1 in/2 cm cubes. Dip in beaten egg and coat with breadcrumbs. Deep fry for 30 seconds, then drain well on kitchen paper, before serving with delicious cranberry sauce.

Serves 4

HOT STILTON AND PEARS

Once the owner of a restaurant, actor *Keith Barron* used to serve delightful English dishes like this unusual sweet and savoury combination of sliced pears on a bed of watercress, covered with Stilton, and flashed under the grill.

watercress
4 ripe pears, peeled, cored and sliced
2 oz/50 g Stilton

Arrange watercress on four flameproof individual serving dishes. Place pear slices on top, then cover with Stilton. Place under a hot grill until Stilton melts and browns.

Serves 4

POTTED SHRIMPS

The best shrimps come from Morecambe, say *Tommy Cannon* and *Bobby Ball*, who both enjoy this quick and easy first course.

4 oz/100 g unsalted butter
8 oz/225 g peeled shrimps
½ tsp cayenne pepper
½ tsp freshly grated nutmeg
salt

Melt butter in a saucepan over a low heat. Reserve about 2 tbsp of melted butter and add shrimps and spices to remainder. Stir until shrimps are coated. Do not overcook. Add salt to taste. Pour into small pots and chill until set. Pour remaining butter over top and chill again until firm. Serve with crusty bread and lettuce.

Serves 4

COQUILLES ST JACQUES

Actress *Ciaran Madden* loves fish. Scallops in a cheesy sauce, served in shells edged with piped, mashed potato are a particular favourite.

2 lb/900 g potatoes, peeled
2 oz/50 g butter
2 tbsp milk
12 fresh or frozen scallops
¼ pint/150 ml dry white wine
1 onion, peeled and chopped
2 oz/50 g mushrooms, wiped and sliced
1 oz/25 g flour
salt and pepper
3 oz/75 g mature Cheddar cheese, grated

Cut potatoes into even-sized pieces. Cook in boiling salted water until soft. Drain. Add 1 oz/ 25 g butter and milk and mash smooth. Cool.

Put mashed potato in a piping bag fitted with a star-shaped nozzle. Scrub 4 scallop shells and dry. Pipe potato in a border of stars around edge.

Wash and dry scallops. Separate orange coral and put to one side. Cut white meat in half and place in a pan with wine. Bring to boil and simmer for 2-3 minutes – no longer or scallops will toughen. Add coral and cook for a further 2 minutes. Remove with a slotted spoon. Top up cooking juices to ½ pint/300 ml with a little milk.

Fry onion in remaining butter until soft. Add mushrooms and flour and cook for 2 minutes. Remove from heat and gradually add wine and milk mixture, stirring continuously. Return to heat and bring to the boil, stirring all the time. Add 2 oz/50 g cheese and seasoning. Simmer for 3 minutes. Stir in scallops.

Spoon mixture into prepared shells. Sprinkle over remaining cheese. Place under a hot grill, until lightly browned and heated through. Garnish with parsley.

Serves 4

ROBBINS PASTA SALAD

A delicious pasta bow and shellfish dish from comedienne *Kate Robbins*.

8 oz/225 g multicoloured pasta shapes
8 oz/225 g jar mussels, drained
4 oz/100 g frozen peeled prawns, defrosted
1 red pepper, de-seeded and cut into strips
2 courgettes, cut into strips

Dressing
3 tbsp olive oil
1 tbsp white wine vinegar
½ tbsp made mustard
1 tbsp parsley, chopped
salt and pepper

Cook pasta in plenty of boiling salted water until just firm to the bite. Drain and cool. Mix with mussels, prawns, pepper and courgettes.

For the dressing, put oil, vinegar, mustard, parsley, salt and pepper in a screw-top jar and shake to blend. Pour over pasta and stir through.

Serves 4

Susie Blake believes that Soup Solitaire is the perfect first course for singles (see page 10).

Sudden Avocado Dip. Everything was 'All Right on the Night' after Denis Norden converted an avocado mousse that flopped into this appetising dish.

POTTED STILTON AND PORT

Mollie Sugden's favourite cheese pâté.

6 oz/150 g Stilton, rind removed
4 tbsp double cream
2 tbsp chopped walnuts
1 tbsp port
squeeze of lemon juice
lemon slice

Mash Stilton with cream. Stir in chopped walnuts, port and lemon juice. Pack into ramekins or an earthenware pot. Decorate with lemon slice. Use as a spread.

Serves 4

SUDDEN AVOCADO DIP

1 unset avocado mousse
4 oz/100 g cream cheese, beaten
5 oz/150 g soured cream, softened
1 clove garlic, crushed
1 small onion, peeled and chopped
few drops tabasco
salt and pepper
whole prawns for garnish
selection of vegetables for crudités, eg, red pepper, courgette, celery, carrot, cauliflower

Beat mousse in a bowl. Stir in cheese, soured cream, garlic, onion, tabasco and seasoning. Pile in a bowl and decorate edge with whole prawns. Cut vegetables into thin strips for dipping.

Serves 6-8

GRAVLAX

Tom Vernon encountered this traditional way of curing salmon on a trip to Sweden.

1 lb/450 g salmon fillet, with skin, sliced in half
1 oz/25 g caster sugar
1 oz/25 g salt
1 oz/25 g sprigs fresh dill
fresh ground black pepper

Dill and honey sauce
4 fl oz/100 ml olive oil
juice of ½ orange
1 tbsp dill, chopped
1 tbsp Dijon mustard
1 tbsp double cream
salt and ground black pepper

Place salmon on a board and rub cut sides with sugar and salt. Place a few dill sprigs on a sheet of foil. Put one piece of salmon skin side down on top of dill. Sprinkle with dill sprigs and pepper, and top with remaining salmon slice, skin side up. Cover with remaining dill. Wrap in foil and place weights on top and marinate in the fridge for 48 hours.

Remove weights and foil. Slice down to the skin at an angle. Serve on a bed of lettuce, with lemon wedges.

Mix sauce ingredients together and pour into a serving dish. Drizzle over sliced salmon before serving.

Serves 4

DRESSED ASPARAGUS

Rory McGrath has a penchant for asparagus.

2×12 oz/350 g tins asparagus, drained

Dressing
3 tbsp olive oil
1 tbsp freshly squeezed lemon juice
½ tsp mustard
salt and pepper
2 oz/50 g pine nuts

Arrange asparagus in a dish. Shake dressing ingredients in a screw-top jar and drizzle over asparagus.

Serves 4

PANCAKE PURSES

An unusual appetiser of pancakes filled with tuna and capers from *Cilla Black*.

Pancakes
4 oz/100 g plain flour
½ tsp salt
1 egg
½ pint/300 ml milk

Filling
7 oz/200 g tin tuna, drained and flaked
1 tbsp capers, chopped
2 tbsp soured cream
8 strands long spaghetti, cooked soft

Sieve flour and salt into a mixing bowl. Make a well in the centre. Add egg and gradually beat in half the milk with a wooden spoon. Whisk in remaining milk. Stand for 20 minutes.

Lightly grease a small frying pan and heat until very hot. Pour enough mix into base of pan to cover thinly. Cook until pancake bubbles underneath, then flip over and cook until brown. Repeat with remaining mixture.

Mix filling ingredients together. Spoon into centre of pancakes. Gather pancakes together to form purses. Tie gently with spaghetti. Eat hot or cold. Re-heat by steaming or by placing in the microwave for 2 minutes on high.

Serves 8

16

SCANDINAVIAN BRUNCH

When we entertain, says Maureen Lipman, I tend to go for a continental theme. We've had quite a few Swedish and Norwegian au pairs over the years and they have introduced us to the delights of Scandinavian cooking. Funnily enough, it's not so very different from traditional Jewish food with lots of cold fish, chicken and pickles.
The family usually eats in the huge kitchen with its view over an enviably wide, lawned garden. This friendly room is fitted with canary yellow cupboards, navy tiles and blue glass lamps. Coincidentally, the colours of the Swedish flag.

SELTINAS

Crisp, shortcrust onion tartlets topped with a rolled anchovy.

8 oz/225 g plain flour
pinch salt
2 oz/50 g margarine
2 oz/50 g lard
water to bind
1 small onion, peeled and sliced
1 oz/25 g butter
¼ pint/150 ml milk
¼ pint/150 ml single cream
2 eggs
salt and pepper
2×2½ oz/65 g tins anchovies

Sieve flour and salt into a bowl. Rub in fat and bind with water to make a dough. Cover and chill in fridge for 30 minutes.

Roll out pastry and cut out circles to line a greased tartlet tin. Fry onion gently in butter until soft. Cool, then spoon into pastry cases. Beat milk, cream, eggs, salt and pepper and pour on top. Cook at Gas 6/400°F/200°C for 20-25 minutes or until golden brown.

Drain and roll anchovies; place on top of tarts 5 minutes before end of cooking time.

Makes 16

BEGGELS

Ping-pong-sized balls of minced chicken and gherkin, dipped in breadcrumbs and grilled.

1 oz/25 g butter
1 oz/25 g flour
8 fl oz/225 ml milk
salt and pepper
12 oz/350 g cooked chicken, skinned and boned
4 oz/100 g gherkins
1 egg
4 oz/100 g wholemeal breadcrumbs

Melt butter in a pan. Add flour and cook for 1 minute. Remove from heat and gradually beat in milk. Return to heat and gradually bring to the boil, stirring all the time. Simmer for 3 minutes. Season, then cool slightly. Put in blender with chicken, gherkins, egg and half breadcrumbs. Blend until smooth. Leave to cool. Roll into balls and coat in remaining crumbs. Brown slightly under grill until golden. Serve hot or cold.

Makes 16

FISCHER

White fish terrine set in a fish-shaped mould, layered with chopped mushrooms.

1½ lb/675 g white fish (cod, whiting, etc)
3 oz/75 g butter, softened
2 eggs, separated
1½ oz/40 g plain flour
4 tbsp single cream
½ tsp dillweed
salt and pepper
¼ pint/150 ml double cream, whipped

Stuffing
4 oz/100 g button mushrooms, wiped and finely chopped
2 oz/50 g butter
2 oz/50 g white breadcrumbs
1 egg, beaten
cucumber slices to decorate mould
2 capers (for eyes)
shredded lettuce

Having removed bones and skin, put fish into a blender with butter, egg yolks, flour, single cream, dillweed and seasoning. Blend until smooth. Fold in double cream. Beat egg whites and fold in. Oil a 1½-2 pint fish mould and spread half the mixture over the bottom.

Fry mushrooms in butter for a few minutes. Stir in breadcrumbs and egg. Spread this on top of mixture in mould. Cover with remaining fish mixture and bake at Gas 3/325°F/160°C for 1 hour 15 minutes or until firm to touch.

Cool in mould. Turn out on a plate and decorate with cucumber slices, capers and lettuce.

Serves 8

FLATTBRÖT

Open sandwiches made from combination of the ingredients below, on rye bread or Swedish toasts.

beetroot slices	lettuce leaves
hard-boiled eggs	smoked mackerel
Swedish cheese	onion rings
cucumber	mackerel fillets
tomato	radishes
mushrooms	

SALMON SALAD

Delicious mixture of salmon and cold vegetables, bound together with lemon mayonnaise.

2×15 oz/425 g tins red salmon, drained, skin and bones removed
6 tomatoes, skinned and chopped
8 oz/200 g cooked, diced potatoes
8 oz/200 g cooked peas
½ cucumber, skin on, diced
1 egg, hard-boiled, quartered

Dressing
6 tbsp mayonnaise
1 tbsp lemon juice
salt and pepper

Place chunks of fish in a bowl. Add tomatoes, potatoes, peas and cucumber. Mix dressing ingredients together and gently stir in. Put into serving bowl and decorate with egg.

Serves 8

STOCKHOLM RICE

Nutty rice with fruit.

1 lb/450 g cooked rice
4 oz/100 g dried apricots, chopped
4 oz/100 g sultanas
4 oz/100 g flaked almonds

Dressing
4 tbsp sunflower oil
1 tbsp white wine vinegar
1 tsp Dijon mustard
salt and pepper

Place cold rice, fruit and nuts in a large bowl. Shake dressing ingredients together in a screw-top jar and stir through rice.

Serves 12

Maureen Lipman prepares a Scandinavian Brunch party in her friendly north London kitchen.

Fish Dishes

Fish and chips may be the dish the British are famed for, but it's strange that we don't make more of the bounty of our shores – especially since we are an island. Today, with the emphasis on healthier eating, this is all beginning to change.

Actress *Ciaran Madden* has always preferred fish to meat and enjoys adventurous ways of preparing it. These are three of her favourites.

SWORDFISH KEBABS

Swordfish is a dense-fleshed fish usually only available in frozen form. But it's filling and perfect for kebabs as the firm meat will not fall apart when cooked. Ask your fishmonger for it.

8 oz/225 g frozen swordfish, defrosted
juice of 1 lemon
2 tbsp olive oil
1 in/2 cm piece of ginger root, peeled and finely
   chopped
salt and pepper
2 small onions, peeled and quartered
8 bay leaves
1 red pepper, de-seeded and cut into squares
4 oz/100 g button mushrooms, wiped
2 courgettes wiped and cut into thick slices
lemon wedges to garnish

Remove skin and any bones from fish. Cut into cubes. Mix lemon juice, oil, ginger root, salt and pepper. Pour over fish and leave to marinate for 1 hour.

Thread fish, vegetables and bay leaf on to long skewers. Brush with marinade, place under hot grill and cook for 6 minutes, turning frequently, or until fish has cooked. Serve with lemon wedges.

Serves 4

MOULES MARINIÈRES

Classic shellfish stew of mussels, onions and garlic, and white wine.

4 lb/1.8 kg live mussels
4 shallots, peeled and finely chopped
2 small cloves garlic, peeled and crushed
1 oz/25 g butter
1 bay leaf
½ pint/300 ml dry white wine
salt and pepper
2 tsp flour mixed into 1 oz/25 g butter
2 tbsp parsley, chopped

Scrub mussels with a stiff brush to clean. Pull off hairy beards and scrape off limpets. Discard broken mussels and any that do not close when tapped smartly with the back of a knife. Put mussels in a large bowl of salted water and soak for an hour. Remove and rinse under cold water.

Fry shallots and garlic in butter, add bay leaf, wine, salt and pepper. Bring to boil, add mussels and cook for 3-4 minutes, shaking pan occasionally, until they open. Discard any mussels that remain closed. Remove mussels from pan with a slotted spoon and place in a large serving dish.

Add flour and butter mixture to pan juices and bring to the boil, stirring until thickened. Add parsley, adjust seasoning, and pour over mussels. Serve with hot crusty bread to dip into juices.

Serves 4

Spaghetti with Clams.

Two-fish Stew

A tasty mix of two haddocks, white and smoked, stewed with shallots and tomatoes.

2 cloves garlic, peeled and crushed
6 shallots, peeled and thinly sliced
2 tbsp olive oil
1 lb/450 g tomatoes, peeled and chopped
1 red pepper, de-seeded and cut into rings
12 oz/350 g white haddock, skinned and cut into chunks
12 oz/350 g smoked haddock, skinned and cut into chunks
8 green olives (optional)
½ pint/300 ml water
1 bay leaf
1 tbsp basil, chopped
salt and pepper
3 whole prawns and basil leaves to garnish

Fry garlic and shallots in oil until soft. Add tomatoes and red pepper and fry for 2 minutes. Add fish, olives, water, bay leaf, basil and seasoning. Bring to boil, then simmer for 5 minutes. Adjust seasoning. Put into serving dish, and garnish with prawns and basil leaves. Serve with mashed potato.

Serves 4

Spaghetti with Clams

Bruce Forsyth's favourite fish and pasta dish pictured above. Use any size clams for this. Use only clams that shut when tapped sharply with the back of a knife. Discard any that remain open. After cooking, discard those that stay closed.

2 tbsp olive oil
1 onion peeled and finely chopped
1 clove garlic, peeled and crushed
15 oz/400 g tin chopped tomatoes
1 tsp sugar
¼ pint/150 ml dry white wine
2 tbsp fresh parsley, chopped
1 tsp dried basil
salt and pepper
8 oz/225 g spaghetti
1 lb/450 g live clams, cleaned and prepared as above

Heat oil and fry onion and garlic until soft. Stir in tomatoes, sugar, wine, 1 tbsp parsley, basil, salt and pepper. Bring to boil and simmer uncovered for 15 minutes until sauce has thickened.

Cook spaghetti in a large pan of boiling salted water for 12 minutes. Drain.

Add clams to tomato sauce and cook until shells open. Stir sauce through spaghetti and garnish with parsley.

Serves 4

SEAFOOD COFFYNES

'Coffynes' is the Old English word for coffins – the shape of the pastry case. This Old English dish comes from the kitchen of *Keith Barron*.

14 oz/400 g puff pastry, rolled out
1 egg, beaten with 1 tbsp water
2 oz/50 g butter
1 tbsp flour
16 fl oz/450 ml fish stock, flavoured with a pinch of
    saffron strands
4 tbsp dry white wine
1 tbsp double cream
8 oz/225 g monkfish or cod, thinly sliced
4 large or 8 small scallops, thinly sliced
4 oz/100 g peeled prawns
parsley sprigs

Cut pastry into four. Score border ½ in/1 cm inside edge and make a pattern on inner oblong. Brush with egg. Bake at Gas 6/400°F/200°C for about 12-15 minutes. Remove lids and inner layer to leave a thin pastry shell. Return to oven for about 2 minutes to dry out.

Melt butter, stir in flour and cook for 1 minute. Gradually add 4 fl oz/100 ml fish stock, wine and cream. Cook gently, stirring, until smooth. Poach fish and scallops in remaining fish stock for 2-3 minutes. Add prawns. Heat through. Drain, then add to sauce.

Reheat coffynes and fill with fish. Replace lids. Garnish with parsley and serve.

Serves 4

EXCLUSIVE

A hot fish dish which is sure to please *Derek Jameson*. Divine chunks of fresh cod with tomatoes, onion and garlic, spiced with whole chillis.

1 onion peeled and chopped
1 clove garlic, crushed
2 tbsp oil
1½ lb/700 g cod, skinned and cut into chunks
4 whole green chillies, trimmed
4 tomatoes, peeled and quartered
¼ pint/150 ml fish stock
salt and freshly ground black pepper
2 tbsp double cream

Fry onion and garlic in oil until soft. Add cod, chillies, tomato, stock and season with salt and pepper. Cover and bring to the boil and simmer until fish flakes. Strain juice into a pan and arrange fish and vegetables in warmed serving dish. Remove chillies. Bring juice to the boil and reduce by half. Stir in cream and pour over fish to serve.

Serves 4

Derek Jameson likes hot and spicy food – to match his news stories.

PAPER BAG SECRET

Cilla Black's surprise is revealed when the paper bag is ripped open. It's trout cooked with vermouth, onion rings, dill and black pepper!

4 small trout, cleaned
4 sprigs dill
salt and pepper
1 small onion, peeled and cut into rings
4 tbsp vermouth
2 oz/50 g butter

Place dill into cavity of each trout, and season with salt and pepper. Put each trout into a greaseproof bag. Add some onion, 1 tbsp vermouth and ½ oz/15 g butter. Seal top of bags. Place on baking tray and cook at Gas 5/375°F/190°C for 15-20 minutes. Tear open bag just before you serve to your guests.

Serves 4

KEITH KIPPER PÂTÉ

KEITH KIPPER PÂTÉ is of course from the kitchen of *Penelope Keith*. A delicious easy snack.

1 lb/450 g cooked kipper fillets, skinned
¼ pint/150 ml double cream
juice of half a lemon
fresh ground black pepper
salt
2 oz/50 g butter
bay leaf
6 whole black peppercorns

Blend the kipper fillets, cream, lemon juice, and salt and pepper in a liquidiser or food processor until smooth. Pack into an earthenware bowl.
    Melt butter over a high heat, then skim off foam. Pour over pâté. Place bay leaf and peppercorns on top for garnish. Serve with crusty French bread.

Serves 2

FITNESS FISH

Bobby Davro attributes his slinky shape to careful eating. Try this fast salmon dish, cooked in the microwave, and served with a low-calorie piquant sauce.

4 salmon cutlets, 1 in/2.5 cm thick
fresh ground black pepper
¼ pint/150 ml natural yoghurt
2 tbsp mint, finely chopped
3 tbsp low-calorie mayonnaise
1 in/2.5 cm piece of cucumber, finely chopped
sprig fresh mint to decorate

Place salmon on a microwave plate with thinner ends pointing inwards. Sprinkle with black pepper, cover and cook on high for 5 minutes. Remove and cool.
    For sauce, mix yoghurt, mint, mayonnaise and cucumber in a bowl. Spoon into a small serving dish and decorate with sprig of mint.
    Arrange salmon on plate and serve with the yoghurt sauce.

Serves 4

FIVERS

The kids will love these home-made fish fingers cut from slabs of cod which *Roy Kinnear* recommends.

14 oz/400 g packet frozen cod steaks
2 oz/50 g flour, seasoned with salt and pepper
1 egg, beaten
4 oz/100 g white breadcrumbs
4 tbsp oil

Defrost and cut each cod steak in half lengthways. Coat in flour, egg, then breadcrumbs. Heat oil in a large pan. Gently fry fish fingers on each side until cooked through and golden. Serve with scoops of mashed potato and peas.

Serves 4

SOUSED HERRINGS

Traditional pickled herrings are a *Bamber Gascoigne* favourite.

4 herrings, cleaned, boned, head and tails removed
salt and pepper
1 onion, finely sliced
1 pint/600 ml spiced pickling vinegar
1 or 2 bay leaves

Open herrings out flat and season with salt and pepper. Spread onions on top. Roll each herring from head to tail and secure with cocktail sticks. Arrange in large ovenproof dish. Pour over vinegar and bake at Gas 3/325°F/160°C for 30 minutes. Leave to cool in vinegar.

Serves 4

Opposite Centurion's Sole – delicate fillets of sole in a white wine and grape sauce.

A traditionalist at heart, Bamber Gascoigne likes old-fashioned recipes. Soused Herrings are a particular favourite.

ALFIE BASS

High-tech. chat-show host *Max Headroom* says, 'Michael Caine, star of 'Alfie', says he loves fish, so I brought back a few memories for him with this.'

2 oz/50 g butter
3-4 lb/1.4-1.8 kg sea bass, cleaned and gutted
salt and pepper
½ in/1 cm root ginger, peeled and chopped
12 spring onions
8 oz/225 g carrots, peeled and cut into strips
2 oz/50 g butter

Butter a large sheet of foil and place fish in centre. Season inside and outside of fish with salt, pepper and ginger. Cut 4 spring onions into strips and sprinkle over fish. Wrap up in foil, place in a large baking tray and cook at Gas 4/350°F/180°C for 40 minutes or until cooked through.

Trim remaining spring onions and cut green end into thin strips lengthways. Leave to curl in cold water. Stir-fry carrots in butter for 5 minutes.

Place fish on serving dish. Garnish with spring onions and carrots.

Serves 6

Centurion's Sole

Delicate fillets of sole in a white wine and grape sauce from *Jimmy Mulville*'s TV persona, the dainty Roman Aulus Paulinus of 'Chelmsford 123'.

2 lemon soles, filleted and skinned
¼ pint/150 ml dry white wine
½ oz/15 g butter
½ oz/15 g flour
½ pint/300 ml milk
salt and white pepper
4 oz/100 g white seedless grapes, washed

Roll up soles and arrange in an ovenproof dish. Pour over wine, cover and bake for 10 minutes at Gas 6/400°F/200°C, or until fish turns opaque. Carefully arrange fish on a serving dish. Pour cooking juices into a jug.

Melt butter in a pan, stir in flour and cook for 1 minute. Remove from heat, and gradually stir in cooking juices and milk. Return to heat, bring to boil, simmer for 3 minutes or until thickened. Season with salt and pepper. Stir in grapes and pour over fish.

Serves 4

Comedy actor *Jimmy Mulville*'s favourite restaurant serves this chunky Zue's fish stew, pictured above, in a tomato and garlic sauce. Or try the delicious pastry Siggies stuffed with mussels and prawns in a creamy shellfish sauce.

Zue's Fish Stew

Filling fish stew packed with firm-fleshed whitefish and shellfish.

1 onion, peeled and finely chopped
1 clove garlic, crushed
1 stick celery, finely chopped
4 tbsp olive oil
1 bay leaf
sprig of parsley
6 tomatoes, skinned, seeded and chopped
1 tbsp tomato purée
12 oz/350 g whitefish, skinned and cut into chunks

4 oz/100 g frozen shelled mussels, defrosted
1 pint/600 ml fish stock
¼ pint/150 ml dry white wine
salt and fresh ground black pepper
6 oz/175 g frozen peeled prawns, defrosted
1 small French loaf, sliced
2 oz/50 g butter
2 cloves garlic, crushed
mustard and cress
whole prawns to garnish

Fry onion, garlic and celery in oil until soft. Add herbs, tomatoes and tomato purée. Cook for 5 minutes. Add fish, mussels, stock and wine. Season. Bring to boil and simmer for 10 minutes. Add prawns and heat through.

Toast bread on one side. Blend butter and garlic. Spread on untoasted side. Grill until butter melts. Serve with stew. Garnish with cress and prawns.

Serves 4

26

SIGGIES

13 oz/375 g frozen puff pastry, defrosted
1 egg, beaten
12 oz/350 g whole prawns
8 oz/225 g frozen shelled mussels, defrosted
1 onion, peeled and chopped
1 stick celery, scrubbed and chopped
1 sprig parsley
1 bay leaf
8 black peppercorns
¼ pint/150 ml dry white wine
¾ pint/425 ml water
2 tsp tomato purée
8 fl oz/225 ml double cream
1 oz/25 g butter in small pieces
1 tbsp brandy
mustard and cress to garnish

Roll out pastry. Cut into 4 oblongs. Score a line ¼ in/0.5 cm inside the edges. Glaze with egg but do not cover the scored line. Cook on a greased baking-sheet in a preheated oven Gas 7/425°F/220°C for 12 minutes. Remove lid with point of a knife, and reserve.

Boil prawn-shells (reserve flesh) with onion, celery, herbs and peppercorns with wine and water for 20 minutes. Strain. Return juice to pan. Boil to reduce by half. Remove from heat, add tomato purée, cream, butter and brandy. Cook gently until slightly thickened. Add prawns and mussels and heat through. Spoon into pastry-shells with remaining sauce around edge. Replace lid. Decorate with cress.

Serves 4

FLAKY PRAWN SLICE

Lovely savoury puff pastry slice from *Mollie Sugden* for a special tea-time treat.

7 oz/200 g pack frozen puff pastry, defrosted
1 egg, beaten
1 oz/25 g butter
1 small onion, peeled and grated
1 oz/25 g flour
½ pint/300 ml milk
salt and pepper
½ tsp dill weed, chopped
4 oz/100 g frozen prawns, defrosted
few whole prawns with shells for decoration
slice of lemon

Roll out pastry on floured board to 10 in/25 cm square. Cut into two equal rectangles. Put on greased baking tray, brush with beaten egg. Leave in fridge for 30 minutes. Cook at Gas 6/400°F/200°C for 15 minutes or until risen and crisp. Cool slightly, remove from trays.

Melt butter in pan, add onion, gently fry until soft. Do not brown. Stir in flour, and cook for a few minutes. Remove from heat and stir in milk. Return to heat and bring slowly to boil, stirring. Simmer for 3-4 minutes, add dill and prawns.

Fill pastry layers with sauce. Serve hot or cold with whole prawns and lemon slice.

Serves 6

A FISHY BUSINESS

Although he usually cooks fish whole in a fish kettle, one of actor, *Oliver Tobias*'s favourite barbecues is a fish one. Sardines and mackerel lend themselves to barbecuing, so does a small whole salmon. And for a special occasion, giant grilled prawns are a great treat. 'We love the idea of barbecuing fish,' says Oliver. 'You get a super crisp skin and delicate moist flesh inside.'

SEA LEGS

Sardines, on a long skewer, barbecued high above the coals.

12 fresh sardines, washed
freshly ground sea salt
1 tbsp fresh parsley, chopped
2 cloves garlic, finely chopped
1 slice lemon, cut into quarters

Season sardines with salt and thread them onto a long metal skewer through their mouths to hang vertically, tails down. Suspend skewered sardines above hot barbecue and cook for about 5-6 minutes, or until lightly browned. Slide fish off skewer, arrange on serving dish and sprinkle with parsley and garlic. Decorate with lemon.

Serves 4

GAMBARAMA

Giant prawns, charcoal-grilled and served with garlic mayonnaise.

8 large prawns

Mayonnaise
salt and freshly ground black pepper
1 egg yolk
1 clove garlic, peeled and crushed
1 tsp vinegar
1/2 tsp mustard
1/4 pint/150 ml sunflower oil

Season prawns with salt and pepper. Grill on barbecue for about 3 minutes each side. Put egg yolk, garlic, vinegar, mustard, salt and pepper in a bowl. Gradually whisk in oil drop by drop until mixture thickens. Increase the flow carefully, whisking continually until all the oil has been added. Serve with prawns.

Serves 4

CAPTAIN'S CUTLASS

Whole fresh salmon, stuffed with onions and fresh herbs, cooked over coals. Delicious!

2½ lb/1 kg whole fresh salmon, gutted and cleaned
salt and pepper
1 onion, peeled, cut into rings
few sprigs dill

Season fish cavity with salt and pepper, and insert onion and some dill. Place on barbecue and cook for 10 minutes each side, or until the fish is cooked through when tested with a skewer. Place on serving plate and decorate with fresh dill. To serve, peel skin away from flesh, and carefully ease from bone. Turn over and repeat on other side. Serve hot, straight from the barbecue, or cold.

Serves 8

TREASURE TROVE

For a refreshing dessert, try these golden slices of juicy pineapple topped with brown sugar, rum and cinnamon, wrapped in foil and grilled.

1 fresh, ripe pineapple
3 tbsp soft brown sugar
¼ pint/150 ml rum
cinnamon

Top and tail pineapple and cut into 8 wedges. Place each wedge on a piece of foil and sprinkle with sugar, rum and a little cinnamon. Wrap up tightly and place on barbecue for 15 minutes. Serve in the foil (to retain the juices), with whipped cream or yoghurt.

Serves 8

BOOTY

Pretty and unusual barbecued vegetables – a delicious accompaniment to these fish dishes.

4 oz/100 g butter, softened
1 tsp grated lemon rind
1 tsp lemon juice
12 oz/350 g baby sweetcorn
4 tomatoes
4 tsp parmesan cheese

Make lemon butter by mixing butter, lemon rind and juice. Mould into a cylindrical shape, wrap in greaseproof paper and chill until hard. Thread sweetcorn onto metal skewers and place on barbecue with tomatoes. Cook for 5 minutes and turn over once during cooking time. Serve topped with parmesan cheese. Cut chilled lemon butter into thick slices and decorate with lemon slice to serve with the vegetables.

Serves 4

SILVER BLADES

Grilled whole mackerel with horseradish sauce.

4 mackerel, gutted and cleaned
salt and freshly ground black pepper
1 small onion, peeled and chopped
1 bunch watercress

Horseradish sauce
1 tbsp grated horseradish
¼ pint/150 ml soured cream
1 tsp lemon juice

For best results, cook mackerel in fish-shaped holders. Season cavities of each fish with salt and pepper, and stuff onion inside. Place mackerel in fish griddles and place on a hot barbecue for 6 minutes each side, or until cooked through. Mix horseradish, soured cream and lemon juice; season with salt and pepper. Remove mackerel from griddles, garnish with watercress and serve with horseradish sauce.

Serves 4

ON THE MOVE

For Judith Chalmers the sight of a picnic hamper conjures up images of moving house. For most people though, changing home is one of the most stressful experiences in life. 'With so much else to think about on moving day,' muses Judith, 'feeding the family often gets forgotten. Children catch the stress of moving too, and it's a good idea to make up a kiddie hamper specially for them.' Not that you need to move house to enjoy a picnic.
'A hamper of food should be be the last thing you load on the removal van – so it is the first thing you take off. Moving always takes far longer than you think.' So whether you are moving house or just having a fun picnic, try some of these recipes for your moveable feast.

HOME SWEET HOME HAMPER

Deep quiche. Eat with tomatoes and cider.

SMOKED MACKEREL QUICHE

10 oz/275 g plain flour
pinch salt
2½ oz/65 g lard
2½ oz/65 g margarine
5-6 tbsp cold water
4 oz/100 g Cheddar cheese, grated
2 smoked mackerel fillets, skinned
4 eggs
¾ pint/425 ml milk
salt and pepper
1 slice tomato

Sift flour and salt into a bowl. Rub in fat. Make a well in the centre and add water. Mix to a soft dough. Knead lightly. Wrap and chill for 30 minutes. Roll out. Line a greased 10 in/25 cm loose-bottomed flan tin. Bake blind at Gas 6/400°F/200°C for 20 minutes. Cool. Place cheese in bottom. Cut mackerel into strips. Arrange in spokes. Beat eggs and milk. Season. Pour into case, top with tomato. Cook at Gas 5/375°F/190°C for 40-45 minutes. Cool.

Serves 6

MOTHER'S MOVING BOX

Cake for coffee time.

CARROT CAKE

2 eggs
2 tbsp oil
1 tbsp natural yoghurt
2 oz/50 g brown sugar
5 oz/150 g self-raising flour
1 level tsp bicarbonate of soda
pinch salt
½ tsp cinnamon
3 oz/75 g chopped nuts
2 oz/50 g desiccated coconut
6 oz/175 g carrot, peeled and grated
4 oz/100 g tinned pineapple, drained and chopped
6 oz/175 g cream cheese
3 oz/75 g icing sugar, sifted
1 tsp lemon juice
5 walnut halves

Beat eggs with oil, yoghurt and sugar until slightly thickened. Sieve flour, bicarbonate, salt and cinnamon together, and fold into mixture. Stir in nuts, coconut, carrots and pineapple. Spoon into a 7 in/18 cm round greased and lined cake tin and bake at Gas 4/350°F/180°C for 1 hour. Cool. Beat cream cheese, icing sugar and lemon juice. Spread on top. Decorate with walnuts.

Serves 8

KIDDIE CASE

Pastry wrapped sausages will keep them happy.
Pack bananas, jellies and orange juice.

TWIZZLE SAUSAGES

7 oz/200 g frozen puff pastry, defrosted
1 lb/450 g sausages
1 egg, beaten

Roll pastry out thinly on a lightly-floured board,
and cut into strips. Wrap a strip around each
sausage and place on a lightly-greased baking
sheet. Brush with egg, and bake at Gas 7/425°F/
220°C for 10-15 minutes, or until pastry is golden.

Serves 4

FRUIT JELLIES

4 oz/100 g seedless green grapes
1 packet lime jelly

Place grapes in four small individual dishes. Make
up jelly according to instructions. Pour over grapes
and leave to set in fridge.

Serves 4

PLOUGHMAN'S PACK

Munch-me pasties. Pack an apple for crunch.

HANKY PIES

4 oz/100 g potatoes, cooked and cut into cubes
4 oz/100 g Cheddar cheese, grated
salt and pepper
13 oz/375 g frozen puff pastry, defrosted
1 egg, beaten

Mix potatoes and cheese. Season with salt and
pepper. Roll out pastry thinly on a lightly-floured
board. Cut into 4 squares. Place filling in centre of
each square. Dampen edges with water, and fold
into parcels, pinching edges together. Place on a
greased baking sheet and brush with egg. Cook at
Gas 7/425°F/220°C for 15 minutes or until golden.

Serves 4

FAMILY FEAST

Home-made chicken liver pâté. Serve with a bottle
of champagne.

CHICKEN LIVER PÂTÉ

Super tasty pâté with crisp crackers and celery.

1 small onion, peeled and chopped
2 cloves garlic, crushed
2 oz/50 g butter
8 oz/225 g chicken livers, washed and trimmed
½ tsp nutmeg
salt and pepper
2 tbsp sherry
2 tbsp single cream

Fry onion and garlic in butter until soft. Add
chicken livers, nutmeg, salt and pepper and sherry
and fry for about 5 minutes. Remove from heat
and stir in cream. Blend until smooth. Spoon into
individual pots. Chill until set.

Serves 4

Poultry Dishes

Always versatile and economical, it's not surprising that chicken finds its way on to most menus every week. But duck and turkey are also readily available, both as the whole bird or in handy portions. Choose from this range of star-studded poultry dishes for a different taste every time.

BODY BLOW

Pasta like this tasty lasagne with chicken livers and ham in a creamy cheese sauce is one of champion boxer *Frank Bruno*'s favourites.

1 large onion, peeled and sliced
1 clove garlic, crushed
3 oz/75 g butter
1 red pepper, de-seeded and sliced
1 lb/450 g chicken livers, picked over and chopped
1 oz/25 g seasoned flour
4 oz/100 g ham, chopped
½ pint/300 ml chicken stock
2 tomatoes, peeled and chopped
salt and pepper
2 oz/50 g plain flour
1½ pints/825 ml milk
6 oz/150 g Cheddar cheese, grated
12 sheets 'no need to pre-cook' lasagne

Gently fry onion and garlic in 1 oz/25 g butter until soft. Add pepper and fry for 3 minutes more. Toss liver in seasoned flour and add to pan. Fry till brown and add ham. Stir in stock and bring to the boil. Add tomatoes and seasoning, then gently simmer for 5 minutes.

Melt remaining butter and add flour. Cook for 1 minute. Gradually add milk. Bring to boil, stirring, till sauce thickens. Add 4 oz/100 g cheese and seasoning.

Butter a 9 in/23 cm square ovenproof lasagne dish. Pour about a quarter of the sauce over the base. Place 4 sheets of lasagne over this. Cover with half the liver mix. Repeat layers, then cover last lasagne layer with sauce. Sprinkle over remaining cheese. Bake at Gas 6/400°F/200°C for 35 minutes until golden.

Serves 4-6

Actress *Trudie Goodwin*, who played WPc June Ackland in 'The Bill' likes chicken cooked slowly as in JAILBIRD, or fast as for HOT PROPERTY.

HOT PROPERTY

Tasty chicken curry delicately flavoured with spices and served with plain rice.

1 tsp turmeric
1 tsp chilli powder
1 tsp ground cumin
1 tsp garam masala
1 in/2.5 cm piece ginger root, peeled and finely chopped
1 clove garlic, crushed
1 tsp salt
4 chicken breasts, boned, skinned and cut into chunks
1 onion, peeled and sliced
1 oz/25 g butter
2 tbsp oil
¼ pint/150 ml water
4 tbsp yoghurt
4 tbsp double cream

Mix spices, garlic and salt. Add chicken and toss until coated. Fry onion in butter and oil until soft. Add chicken and fry until lightly browned. Pour in water and simmer for 5 minutes. Stir in yoghurt and cream. Reheat gently without boiling.

Serves 4

JAILBIRD

Whole chicken cooked with onions, garlic and olives with streaky bacon tucked over the breast, which is meltingly tender and flavourful after slow cooking.

3 rashers streaky bacon, derinded
3 lb/1.4 kg fresh chicken, wiped
2 tbsp olive oil
2 onions, peeled and chopped
2 cloves garlic, peeled and crushed
4 tomatoes, peeled
3 oz/75 g black olives
½ pint/300 ml chicken stock
salt and ground black pepper

Lay bacon across chicken. Heat oil and cook onions and garlic until soft. Spoon into an ovenproof casserole and place chicken on top. Arrange tomatoes and olives around chicken, pour over stock and season with salt and pepper. Cover and cook at Gas 2/300°F/150°C for 4-6 hours, or until tender.

Serves 4

UNEXPECTED CHICKEN SALAD

Scrumptious chicken salad concocted for *Denis Norden* when what should have been a straightforward roast chicken came out of the oven a complete and utter wreck.

3 lb/1.4 kg overcooked chicken, skinned and boned
¼ pint/150 ml mayonnaise
juice of 1 lemon
salt and pepper
8 oz/225 g tin pineapple rings, cut into pieces and
   drained
2 oz/50 g peanuts
watercress for garnish

Cut chicken into chunks. Mix with mayonnaise, lemon juice, salt and pepper, pineapple and peanuts. Garnish with watercress and serve with a crisp salad.

Serves 4

Denis Norden can turn these disasters into delights. See pages 9, 15 and 89 for more recipes.

BELLY-ACHE PIE

In spite of the name this dish from *Roy Kinnear* is a corker of a pie with tender chicken and ham with peas in a creamy sauce, topped with golden puff pastry.

3 oz/75 g butter
3 oz/75 g flour
1½ pints/850 ml milk
salt and pepper
1½ lb/700 g cooked chicken, diced
8 oz/225 g cooked ham, diced
4 oz/100 g frozen peas, defrosted
13 oz/375 g packet puff pastry, defrosted
1 egg, beaten

Melt butter in a large pan. Stir in flour and cook for 2 minutes. Remove from heat and gradually stir in milk. Return to heat and gradually bring to boil. Simmer for 3-4 minutes until thickened. Season and stir in chicken, ham and peas. Spoon into an ovenproof dish. Cool.

Roll out pastry thinly to fit top. Cut a ½ in/ 1 cm-wide strip of pastry. Place around edge of pie dish, and dampen with water. Lay pastry lid over rim and trim edges. Seal edges. Cut out leaves from pastry trimmings and dampen to secure. Brush pie at Gas 6/400°F/200°C for 30 minutes, or until pastry is golden.

Serves 6-8

Susan Penhaligon likes to cook casseroles long and slow – often all day – so she always has a hot meal ready in the oven when she comes home. Try one of these two delicious all-in-one dishes.

CHICKEN AND PEPPERS

Colourful tasty chicken dish with a flavour of the south of France.

4 chicken joints
seasoned flour
4 tbsp oil
2 medium onions, peeled and sliced
2 cloves garlic, crushed
1 green pepper, de-seeded and sliced thinly
1 red pepper, de-seeded and cut into strips
14 oz/400 g can tomatoes
½ pint/300 ml red wine
¼ pint/150 ml chicken stock
1 tsp oregano
1 bay leaf
2 oz/50 g black olives, pitted

Dip chicken joints in seasoned flour. Heat oil in a large flameproof casserole. Fry onions and garlic until soft. Add chicken joints and brown on all sides. Add peppers, tomatoes, wine, stock, oregano and bay leaf and simmer gently for 40 minutes. Sprinkle black olives over the top before serving.

Serves 4

CASSOULET WITH DUCK

Substantial and filling dish of beans with duck.

2 medium onions, peeled and sliced
3 tbsp oil
2 garlic cloves, crushed
1 lb/450 g tomatoes, chopped
1 tbsp tomato purée
1 tbsp black treacle
½ pint/300 ml beef stock
salt and pepper
6 oz/175 g bacon, derinded and diced
4 duck portions
1 oz/25 g butter
14 oz/400 g tin haricot beans

Drain beans. Fry onion in oil until soft. Add garlic, tomatoes, purée, treacle, stock, salt and pepper. Bring to boil and simmer for 5 minutes. Stir in beans. Fry bacon and duck portions in butter over a low heat until browned. Place in casserole and cook at Gas 4/350°F/180°C for 1½ hours. Skim off fat. Add beans and heat through.

Serves 4

Cassoulet with Duck.

STOP PRESS

Stop what you're doing and press green peppercorns into skinned chicken breast fillets to make the dish with more than a touch of spice from *Derek Jameson*'s kitchen. Cheap, but unusual and good enough for a dinner party.

4 chicken fillets, skinned
1 tbsp green peppercorns
salt
2 tbsp oil
¼ pint/150 ml double cream

Remove bone from underneath chicken breast, leaving leg bone intact. Press peppercorns into flesh on both sides. Season with salt and fry in oil until cooked through. Stir in cream and cook for 1 minute before serving.

Serves 4

Chicken is such a versatile bird. Actress *Joan Blackham* of ITV's sitcom 'Home to Roost' finds she uses it in stocks and soups as well as for straightforward chicken dishes, like the six which follow.

CHICKEN À L'ORANGE

Unusual and delicious dish with a tangy flavour.

4 chicken quarters
2 tbsp oil
1 oz/25 g butter
½ oz/15 g flour
¼ pint/150 ml chicken stock
juice of 1 orange
1 tsp grated orange rind
salt and pepper
orange slices, to decorate

Fry chicken in oil and butter until browned. Remove to a casserole dish. Stir flour into cooking juices in pan. Gradually add stock, orange juice and rind. Bring to boil and pour over chicken. Season. Cook at Gas 5/375°F/190°C for 1½ hours. Decorate with orange slices before serving on a bed of blanched baby courgettes.

Serves 4

CHICKEN CARIBBEAN

Cold chicken salad, spiked with a touch of curry. Super for a quick lunch, or a buffet dish.

12 oz/350 g cooked chicken, skinned and cut into
  chunks
3 tbsp mayonnaise
2 tbsp natural yoghurt
grated rind of ½ lemon
1 tsp curry paste
1 bunch spring onions, trimmed and sliced
1 red apple, cored and cut into chunks
2 oz/50 g toasted flaked almonds
2 pineapple rings, cut into chunks
salt and pepper
4 lettuce leaves

Put chicken in a large bowl. Mix mayonnaise, yoghurt, lemon rind and curry paste until smooth. Stir into chicken with spring onions, apple, half the toasted almonds, and pineapple. Season with salt and pepper. Place lettuce in a serving dish and spoon over chicken mixture. Sprinkle over remaining almonds.

Serves 4

CHICKEN KIEV

Chicken breast stuffed with garlic and parsley butter, coated in breadcrumbs and deep-fried. Cut into it and a fragrant pool of garlic butter flows on to the plate.

4 oz/100 g butter, softened
5 cloves garlic, crushed
1 tbsp parsley, chopped
ground black pepper
4 chicken breasts, trimmed
2 oz/50 g seasoned flour
2 eggs, beaten
4 oz/100 g fresh white breadcrumbs
oil for deep-frying
sliced tomato
watercress, to garnish

Mash butter with garlic and parsley. Season with pepper. Mould into 4 sausage shapes and chill until hard. Make a slit down one side of each chicken breast, and insert butter. Secure edges with cocktail sticks. Dip carefully in flour, then egg, then breadcrumbs to coat. Chill for 45 minutes. Deep-fry in a large pan of oil until golden brown and cooked through. Garnish with tomato and watercress.

Serves 4

CHICKEN WITH LEMON AND TARRAGON

Joan Blackham raises her glass to Chicken with Lemon and Tarragon.

Tarragon is the perfect herb to use with chicken. Add lemon, and the combination is superb.

3 lb/1.4 kg fresh chicken, without giblets
1 lemon, wiped and sliced
1 tsp mixed herbs
1 onion, peeled
1 oz/25 g butter
1 tbsp tarragon
salt and pepper
parsley, to garnish

Wipe chicken inside and out. Put lemon, mixed herbs and onion into main cavity. Place in a roasting tin and dot butter on top. Sprinkle over tarragon, and season with salt and pepper. Roast at Gas 5/375°F/190°C for 1½ hours, or until golden and juices run clear when pierced with a skewer. Garnish with parsley, and serve with roast potatoes and carrots.

Serves 4

Coq au Vin

Classic French dinner party dish which is always the right choice.

4 chicken portions
2 tbsp oil
1 oz/25 g butter
1 onion, peeled and sliced
1 clove garlic, crushed
½ oz/15 g flour
½ pint/300 ml red wine
1 bay leaf
1 bouquet garni
salt and fresh ground pepper
4 oz/100 g button mushrooms, wiped
chopped parsley, to garnish

Fry chicken in oil and butter until browned. Remove and place in a casserole dish. Add onion and garlic to pan and fry until soft. Stir in flour and gradually add wine. Pour over chicken, add bay leaf and bouquet garni and season with salt and pepper. Cover and cook at Gas 4/350°F/180°C for 1 hour 15 minutes. Remove from oven and add mushrooms, cook for a further 15 minutes. Discard bay leaf and bouquet garni and garnish with parsley.

Serves 4

Chicken Véronique

Delicious dish of chicken in a white wine sauce with green grapes.

4 chicken supremes, skinned
¼ pint/150 ml chicken stock
1 bay leaf
½ onion, peeled and stuck with cloves
½ oz/15 g butter
½ oz/15 g flour
¼ pint/150 ml milk
salt and pepper
4 oz/100 g seedless white grapes
watercress, to garnish

Place chicken in an ovenproof dish. Pour over stock and add bay leaf and onion. Cover and cook for 30 minutes at Gas 5/375°F/190°C until chicken is cooked. Strain juice into a jug, discarding bay leaf and onion. Keep chicken warm in oven while making sauce.

Melt butter, stir in flour and cook for 1 minute. Remove from heat and gradually add reserved stock and milk. Return to heat and bring to the boil, stirring. Simmer for 3-4 minutes, season. Pour over chicken and decorate with grapes and watercress.

Serves 4

Turkey in Chocolate Sauce

'This unusual dish is a Mexican speciality,' says well-travelled *Anneka Rice*. Turkey in chocolate sauce? It may sound peculiar, but it is absolutely delicious. The chocolate adds a subtle richness and colour to the sauce – but no one will ever guess what it really is.

4 lb/1.8 kg frozen turkey, thawed
juice of half a lemon
2 tbsp dark brown sugar
salt and pepper
oil for frying
parsley, to garnish

Sauce
2 tbsp oil
2 onions, peeled and finely chopped
2 cloves garlic, crushed
2 oz/50 g seedless raisins
½ tsp mixed spice
½ tsp cinnamon
½ tsp chilli powder, or to taste
1 oz/25 g chocolate, broken into squares
14 oz/400 g tin chopped tomatoes

Remove meat from turkey bones and cut into chunks. Sprinkle with lemon juice, sugar, salt and pepper. Marinate for 1 hour. Fry in small batches in oil until browned and put to one side.

For the sauce, heat oil in a large pan and fry onions and garlic until soft. Add remaining sauce ingredients and bring to the boil. Allow to boil until reduced by a third, then liquidise. Return to pan, add turkey chunks, and heat through. Adjust seasoning. Garnish with parsley.

Serves 4

OUT FOR A DUCK

When *Bernard Braden* arrived in England 38 years ago he was a meat and potatoes man. His only taste of exotic foreign foods was at the Chinese restaurants in his home town of Vancouver, Canada.

Today, Braden's favourite Chinese restaurant is Dynasty in London's Finchley Road. Run by Mr Wu, this restaurant specialises in Sichuan and Peking dishes such as Crispy Duck and Prawns in Hot Garlic Sauce. The trouble is that diners are spoilt for choice. Most Chinese restaurants have such a vast menu that the average person doesn't quite know where to start. Bernard's advice is always to go for the set meal. Most restaurants have one. And the great thing is it's fast, usually well-priced and, most importantly, well-balanced.

CHICKEN WITH CASHEW NUTS

A Chinese dish with a lovely mix of tender chicken and crunchy cashews with a yellow bean sauce which *Bernard Braden* often chooses.

1 egg white
pinch of salt
2 tsp cornflour
4 chicken fillets, skinned and diced
4 tbsp oil
3 oz/75 g cashew nuts
2 tbsp yellow bean sauce
1 tbsp dry sherry
1 tbsp soy sauce
cucumber slices for garnish

Mix egg white, salt and cornflour. Dip chicken pieces in to coat, then leave in fridge for 15 minutes. Heat 3 tbsp oil until medium hot. Add chicken pieces and stir-fry until they turn white. Remove from pan with a slotted spoon. Drain oil, then replace with another tablespoon of oil. Fry cashew nuts quickly. Add yellow bean sauce, sherry and soy sauce. Add cooked chicken to pan and stir to reheat for 2 minutes. Garnish with cucumber and serve immediately.

Serves 6

CRISPY SICHUAN DUCK

Traditional crispy Chinese duck eaten wrapped in thin pancakes with matchstick cucumber slices, spring onions and hoisin sauce, available in supermarkets.

3½ lb/1.6 kg duck
2 tbsp five-spice powder
salt
½ in/1 cm root ginger, sliced
4 spring onions, chopped
2 pints/1.2 litres groundnut oil

Wipe duck thoroughly. Rub inside and out with five-spice and salt. Wrap in foil and leave in fridge for 2-3 hours.

Put ginger and spring onions in duck cavity. Place duck on a trivet and immerse in a steamer with 2 in/5 cm boiling water. Steam gently for 2 hours, topping up water if necessary.

Remove duck from steamer. Discard ginger and onions. Cool thoroughly, then leave duck to dry in fridge.

Just before serving cut duck into quarters and deep-fry until crispy. Drain on kitchen paper and serve with pancakes, hoisin sauce, cucumber and spring onions.

Serves 6

PANCAKES

10 oz/275 g plain flour
9 fl oz/275 ml boiling water
2 tbsp sesame oil

Sift flour into a large bowl. Stir in water gradually
to make a pliable dough. Knead smooth. Cover
bowl and rest for 30 minutes. Knead again. When
dough is smooth, nip off marble-sized lumps.
Flatten into rounds. Place one round on a floured
work surface, paint with sesame oil, then place a
second round on top. Roll out the two together
until 4 in/10 cm in diameter. Heat a little oil in a
pan and cook the double pancake on both sides.
Peel apart. Repeat until all the dough is used up.
Keep pancakes warm in a strainer inside a cloth-
covered steamer.

SWEET AND SOUR PORK

Dish of mixed tastes, cooked in a wok.

12 oz/350 g pork fillet, in small cubes
4 tbsp oil
2 oz/50 g pineapple, chopped
4 spring onions, sliced
3 tbsp tomato ketchup
2 tbsp sherry
2 tsp sugar
6 tbsp cider vinegar
1 tbsp cornflour
cucumber for garnish

Quickly fry pork in oil for 3-4 minutes. Remove
from wok. Add pineapple and onions to wok and
stir-fry for 2 minutes. Add ketchup, sherry and
sugar, and stir well. Mix cider vinegar into
cornflour and add to wok. Stir for 2-3 minutes
until sauce thickens. Garnish with cucumber.

Serves 6

SEAWEED

An appetiser which isn't seaweed at all but deep-
fried shredded cabbage or kale.

1 lb/450 g kale or spring greens, washed, dried and
    trimmed of coarse stalks
oil for deep frying
3 tsp sugar
1 tsp salt
tomato slices for garnish

Place leaves on top of each other. Roll up tightly to
make a cylinder shape. Cut into thin shreds. Heat
oil and deep-fry cabbage shreds very quickly.
Remove them as soon as they rise to the surface.
Sprinkle sugar and salt to taste. Garnish with
tomato slices.

Serves 6

Meat Dishes

Mouth-watering roasts, stews and richly-flavoured casseroles have always been Great British favourites. Whether you choose to try a quick-midweek cheapie like Lancashire Hotpot, or special occasion dinners such as Boeuf en Croute, these meaty celebrity dishes will be sure to please.

Comedy duo *Hale and Pace* – the Two Rons of the Channel Four series 'The Management' – are rather partial to hefty meat dishes like these three.

BRUISERS

Tender chunks of beef and kidney with an overhanging crisp puff pastry crust. Make one for each person.

1 large onion, peeled and sliced
2 tbsp oil
1½ lb/700 g chuck steak, diced
4 lambs' kidneys, trimmed and diced
1 oz/25 g seasoned flour
½ pint/300 ml beef stock
¼ pint/150 ml red wine
1 bay leaf
salt and pepper
4 oz/100 g button mushrooms, wiped and sliced
13 oz/375 g pack frozen puff pastry, defrosted
1 egg, beaten

Fry onion in oil until soft. Toss steak and kidney in seasoned flour and fry with onion until browned on all sides. Gradually add stock and wine, stirring all the time. Add bay leaf; season with salt and pepper. Bring to the boil, cover and simmer for 1½ hours or until steak is tender. Stir in mushrooms and cook for a further 10 minutes. Leave to cool.

Fill four individual pie dishes. Roll out pastry on a lightly-floured board and cut out tops to fit pie dishes. Dampen edges of dishes with water and lay pastry on top. Brush pastry with egg and bake at Gas 7/425°F/220°C for 20 minutes or until pastry is puffed and golden.

Makes 4

Double-act comics Hale and Pace sample the perfect combination of steak and kidney in Bruisers.

BOUNCERS' BOILED BEEF

Delicious beef cooked slowly with whole carrots and dumplings.

3 lb/1.4 kg silverside of beef
2 leeks, sliced and washed
1 large onion, peeled and sliced
1 small turnip, peeled and diced
1 bouquet garni
2 bay leaves
2 lb/900 g carrots, peeled and cut into sticks
salt and pepper

Dumplings
4 oz/100 g self-raising flour
pinch salt
1 tsp dried thyme
2 oz/50 g beef suet
2-3 tbsp water

Place beef in large pan. Cover with water and bring to the boil. Simmer for 1½ hours. Add leeks, onion, turnip, bouquet garni and bay leaves. Cook for 45 minutes. Add carrots and seasoning and cook for a further 30 minutes.
  For dumplings, sift flour and salt into a bowl. Stir in thyme and suet. Mix to a soft dough with water. Mould into small dumplings. Remove lid and add to beef 20 minutes before end of cooking time.

Serves 4

BUNCH OF FIVES

Make the mash interesting by flavouring it with onion.

3 lb/1.4 kg potatoes, peeled and cut into even-sized
  chunks
1 small onion, peeled and chopped
1 oz/25 g butter
4 tbsp milk
salt and fresh ground black pepper
2 lb/900 g large pork sausages

Cook potatoes in boiling salted water for 20 minutes. Drain and mash. Add onion, butter, milk and seasoning. Grill or fry sausages brown. Serve with mash.

Serves 4

Ray Brooks enjoys a pint and a meal in his favourite pub. These are three of landlady Miriam's specialities.

MIRIAM'S CHILLI

Hot stuff that bites back!

1 large onion, peeled and sliced
2 cloves garlic, crushed
1 oz/25 g butter
1 lb/450 g minced beef
1 oz/25 g brown sugar
4 tbsp tomato purée
14 oz/400 g tin tomatoes
2-3 tsp chilli powder, according to taste
½ tsp cumin powder
salt and pepper
1 bay leaf
15 oz/425 g can kidney beans

Fry onion and garlic until soft in butter. Add mince and fry until brown. Add sugar and tomato purée and fry for 2 minutes. Stir in tomatoes, chilli powder, cumin and bay leaf, then season. Bring to boil and simmer for 45 minutes, stirring. Remove bay leaf, stir in beans. Serve with rice.

Serves 4

KEW BRIDGE MOUSSAKA

Traditional recipe, perfected on the banks of the Thames.

3 aubergines, thinly sliced
1 clove garlic, crushed
1 onion, peeled and sliced
1 oz/25 g butter
1 lb/450 g minced lamb,
1 tbsp tomato purée
1 bay leaf
14 oz/400 g tin tomatoes
salt and pepper
1 oz/25 g butter
1 oz/25 g flour
½ pint/300 ml milk
¼ pint/150 ml Greek yoghurt
pinch nutmeg
6 oz/175 g Cheddar cheese, grated

Soak aubergines in bowl of salted water for 30 minutes. Rinse and drain, then blanch for 2

Ray Brooks tucks into a bowlful of landlady Miriam's Kew Bridge Moussaka.

minutes. Blot on kitchen paper. Fry garlic and onion in butter. Add lamb and fry until browned. Stir in tomato purée, bay leaf and tomatoes. Season, bring to boil, and simmer uncovered for 30 minutes, stirring. Make a white sauce: melt butter in pan. Add flour and cook for 2 minutes. Remove from heat and gradually stir in milk. Return to heat and bring to the boil, stirring continuously. Simmer until thickened. Take off heat, stir in yoghurt, nutmeg, 4 oz/100 g cheese and season. Butter a 3 pint/1.7 litre ovenproof dish. Place half meat mix on the base. Add a layer of aubergines. Repeat and pour over sauce. Sprinkle with cheese. Bake at Gas 6/400°F/200°C for 45 minutes.

Serves 4

WHYBROW'S PIE

Light flaky pastry crust, over tender chunks of steak and kidney with mushrooms.

1 large onion, peeled and sliced
1 oz/25 g butter
1 lb/450 g stewing steak, trimmed and cut into 1 in/ 2 cm cubes
8 oz/225 g beef kidney, cut into small pieces
1 oz/25 g plain flour
½ pint/300 ml beef stock
dash Worcester sauce
salt and pepper
4 oz/100 g button mushrooms, wiped and sliced
7½ oz/200 g packet puff pastry, defrosted
1 tbsp flour, 1 egg, beaten

Fry onion in butter until soft. Add steak and kidney and cook until browned. Stir in flour and cook for 2 minutes. Gradually add stock, sauce and seasoning. Bring to boil and simmer for 1½ hours. Add mushrooms and cook for 15 minutes more. Pour into pie dish and cool. Roll out pastry on a lightly floured board. Cut off a thin strip and fit around edge of dish. Dampen with water, then cover pie with pastry, pinching edges to seal. Pierce hole for steam. Decorate with pastry leaves from trimmings. Glaze with egg. Bake at Gas 7/ 425°F/220°C for 30-35 minutes or until risen and golden.

Serves 4

Three meaty dishes from *Susan Penhaligon*'s collection of casserole recipes.

GOULASH PENHALIGON

Rich, paprika-red pork stew with caraway seeds.

2 tbsp oil
2 rashers bacon, de-rinded and chopped
1 onion, peeled and chopped
1½ lb/700 g lean pork, cubed
1 tbsp flour
2 tbsp paprika
¾ pint/425 ml beef stock
2-3 tsp caraway seeds
1 tbsp tomato purée
salt and fresh black pepper
¼ pint/150 ml soured cream
1 tbsp fresh chopped parsley

Heat oil in a large pan, add bacon and onion and cook for 2 minutes. Add pork and fry quickly to seal. Mix in flour, paprika, stock, caraway seeds, tomato purée and seasoning. Cover and simmer gently for 1 hour. Swirl soured cream on top, then sprinkle with chopped parsley before serving.

Serves 4

LAMB MAHAL

Mild and creamy curry, flavoured with spices and ground almonds.

1 oz/25 g butter
1 clove garlic, crushed
1 onion, peeled and sliced
1 green pepper, de-seeded and thinly sliced
½ tsp ground turmeric
½ tsp ground coriander
½ tsp ground cumin
½ tsp ground ginger
1½ lb/700 g lean lamb, trimmed and cubed
¾ pint/425 ml chicken stock
2 oz/50 g ground almonds

Melt butter in a large pan. Add garlic, onion, pepper and cook until soft. Stir in spices and cook for 1 minute. Add lamb and cook for further 2-3 minutes to brown. Pour in stock and simmer for 20 minutes, adding extra liquid if necessary. Add almonds, stir and reheat. Serve with rice and cucumber raita.

Serves 4

BEEF IN RED WINE

Dark and interesting beef casserole with button mushrooms and shallots.

1 tbsp oil
2 rashers bacon, de-rinded and chopped
1½ lb/700 g chuck steak, cubed
1 clove garlic, crushed
1 tbsp flour
½ pint/300 ml red wine
¼ pint/150 ml beef stock
bouquet garni
12 shallots, peeled
4 oz/100 g button mushrooms, wiped
2 slices bread, toasted and cut into triangles
2 tbsp fresh chopped parsley

Heat oil in a large pan and fry bacon. Add steak and cook until browned on all sides. Remove and keep warm. Add garlic to the pan and fry gently. Stir in flour. Remove from heat and pour in wine and stock. Transfer to a casserole. Add bouquet garni, cover and cook for 1 hour at Gas 5/375°F/190°C or until meat is tender. Add shallots and mushrooms 20 minutes before end of cooking time. Remove bouquet garni before serving. Dip toast triangle tips into beef juices, then into chopped parsley to garnish.

Serves 4

STONE AGE LAMB

Like the character he played in 'Chelmsford 123' (Badvoc, the uncouth and hairy Celt) *Rory McGrath* likes a touch of the unusual. This leg of lamb is served with plum sauce.

4 lb/1.8 kg leg of lamb
2 cloves garlic, bruised
salt and pepper

Plum sauce
1 small onion, peeled and finely chopped
2 tbsp olive oil
6 red plums, chopped and stoned
1 tbsp white wine vinegar
½ pint/300 ml red wine
sprig of thyme
2 tbsp brown sugar
1 oz/25 g raisins, chopped
salt and fresh ground black pepper
watercress to garnish

Place lamb in a roasting tin. Rub skin with garlic and season with salt and pepper. Roast in oven at Gas 5/375°F/190°C for about 2 hours.

For sauce, gently fry onion in oil until soft. Add plums, vinegar, wine, thyme, sugar and raisins. Bring to the boil and simmer for 15 minutes. Remove thyme, and blend until smooth. Season with salt and pepper. Serve hot or cold with lamb. Garnish with watercress.

Serves 4

Bouncer's Boiled Beef (see page 42).

SPORTS PAGE

Energy-packed stew gingered up for the best results, for *Derek Jameson*.

1 onion, peeled and sliced
2 in/5 cm piece ginger root, peeled and cut into thin
    slices
2 tbsp oil
1½ lb/700 g pork, trimmed and cubed
1 oz/25 g seasoned flour
½ pint/300 ml chicken stock
red pepper, de-seeded and cut into chunks
4 oz/100 g button mushrooms, wiped and trimmed
salt and freshly ground black pepper

Fry onion and ginger in oil. Remove with a slotted spoon. Coat pork in flour and add to pan. Fry until browned an all sides. Return onion and ginger and pour over stock.

Bring to the boil, stirring all the time, for 1½ hours or until pork is tender. Add pepper and mushrooms, and season with salt and pepper. Cook for a further 15 minutes.

Serves 4

LEG OF LAMB WITH FLAGEOLET BEANS

Fragrant and tender lamb – the beans soak up the the juices. This is *Prunella Scales*'s choice.

4 lb/1.8 kg leg of lamb
salt and fresh ground black pepper
8 oz/225 g flageolet beans, soaked overnight in cold
    water

Season lamb with salt and pepper; place in a roasting tin and roast at Gas 4/350°F/180°C for 2½ hours. Baste with juices.

Drain beans; place in a large pan and cover with water. Bring to a rolling boil for at least 10 minutes. Reduce heat, simmer for 35-40 minutes, or until tender. Drain and season. Place on a warmed platter and put lamb on top. Decorate with rosemary.

Serves 6

PORKÖLT

Travelling gourmet *Tom Vernon* loves a hearty Hungarian goulash to remind him of his visit there.

1 large onion, peeled and sliced
2 cloves garlic, crushed
2 tbsp oil
2 lb/900 g stewing steak, trimmed and cut into cubes
2 tbsp seasoned flour
1 tbsp paprika
6 tomatoes, peeled and chopped
1 red pepper, cut into rings and de-seeded
8 new potatoes, peeled
¾ pt/425 ml red wine
salt and ground black pepper
4 tbsp soured cream
1 tsp parsley, chopped

Fry onion and garlic in oil until soft. Toss steak in seasoned flour, add to pan and fry until browned. Stir in paprika, tomatoes, red pepper, potatoes and wine. Season with salt and pepper, cover and cook slowly on top of oven for 2 hours or until meat is tender, adding extra wine if necessary. Serve with a swirl of cream and parsley.

Serves 4

It's not surprising that Lancashire born comedy duo, *Cannon and Ball*, love the food of the north. Here are a few of their favourites.

MEAT PIE CANNON

Cheap, filling and tasty pie with a layer of sliced potatoes in the middle.

1 large onion, peeled and sliced
4 carrots, peeled and diced
4 sticks celery, chopped
1 turnip, peeled and diced
3 tbsp oil
1½ lb/700 g stewing steak, trimmed and cubed
½ pint/300 ml beef stock
1 bay leaf
salt and pepper
1 lb/450 g potatoes, peeled, thickly sliced, and boiled
13 oz/375 g packet puff pastry
1 egg, beaten

Fry onion, carrots, celery and turnip in oil for a few minutes. Add meat and fry until browned. Pour over stock, add bay leaf, salt and pepper. Bring to the boil and simmer for 2 hours, stirring occasionally. Allow to cool.

Place half the meat mixture in a pie dish. Add a layer of potatoes. Pour remaining mixture on top.

Roll out pastry on a lightly floured top. Cut strips of pastry to cover rim of dish and dampen. Lay pastry on top, seal and trim. Pinch edges together. Pierce pastry top with three holes, using a skewer. Glaze with beaten egg. Cook at Gas 6/ 400°F/200°C for 30 minutes or until well risen and golden brown.

Serves 4

SHIRT-LAP PUDDING

So-called because the tails of worn-out shirts were used to wrap this for steaming! Use foil today.

1 onion, peeled and chopped
1 oz/25 g butter
1 lb/450 g minced beef
½ tsp oregano
salt and freshly ground black pepper
8 oz/225 g self-raising flour
4 oz/100 g suet
large pinch salt
1 tbsp fresh chopped parsley
8 tbsp water
watercress for garnish

Fry onion in butter until soft. Add mince and fry until browned. Add oregano and seasoning, and gently fry for 20 minutes more. Cool.

Put flour, suet, salt and parsley in a bowl and mix to a soft dough with water. Roll out on a lightly floured surface to a 12 in/30 cm square. Brush edges with water.

Spread filling over pastry, leaving a 1 in/2 cm border. Loosely roll up pastry like a Swiss roll. Seal edges, wrap loosely in foil and screw the ends tightly. Lower into boiling water and boil gently for 2½ hours, topping up water as necessary. Unwrap carefully. Serve garnished with watercress.

Serves 6

Lancashire-born Cannon and Ball naturally love Hot Pot.

LANCASHIRE HOT POT

Traditional dish from Lancashire with tender lamb topped with golden potato slices.

3 lb/1.4 kg best end of neck lamp chops, trimmed of fat
1 tsp salt
freshly ground black pepper
1 lb/450 g onions, peeled and thinly sliced
2 lb/900 g potatoes, peeled and thickly sliced
1 pint/600 ml beef stock
1 oz/25 g butter

Place chops in a layer in the bottom of an ovenproof dish. Sprinkle with salt and pepper. Add a layer of onions, potatoes and season again. Repeat until lamb, onion and potatoes have all been used, ending with a layer of potatoes. Pour over stock and dot top with butter. Cover and cook at Gas 3/325°F/160°C for about 2 hours. Remove lid and cook until potato browns.

Serves 6

BOBBY'S LOBBY

A tasty meat and potato hash.

1 onion, peeled and chopped
1 oz/25 g butter
1 lb/450 g minced beef
1½ lb/700 g potatoes, peeled and diced
dash of Worcestershire sauce
salt and pepper

Fry onion in butter until soft. Add mince and fry until browned. Add potatoes, sauce, salt and pepper. Cook for 30 minutes, stirring occasionally.

Serves 4

'Bullseye'-host *Jim Bowen* adores steak in any form. Here are just a few of his favourite recipes.

PEPPER STEAKS

Tender sirloin steaks studded with peppercorns for those with a taste for a touch of heat.

1 tbsp green peppercorns
4 × 6 oz/175 g sirloin steaks, fat trimmed
salt and pepper
2 tbsp oil
¼ pint/150 ml double cream
1 tbsp parsley, chopped

Crush peppercorns and press into steaks on both sides. Season with salt and pepper. Heat oil in a large frying pan, add steaks and cook according to taste. Pour over cream and heat through. Arrange on a serving plate and garnish with parsley.

Serves 4

STEAK TARTARE

Made from flavoured raw minced fillet steak – unusual but very tasty.

1 lb/450 g fillet steak
1 onion, peeled and finely chopped
1 tbsp capers, chopped
1 tbsp parsley, chopped
½ tsp fresh thyme, chopped
2 large eggs, beaten
1 tsp Worcestershire sauce
pinch mustard powder
salt and pepper
8 anchovy fillets
2 tomatoes, sliced
4 lettuce leaves
1 onion, peeled and cut into rings

Mince steak and place in a large bowl. Add onion, capers, parsley, thyme, eggs, Worcestershire sauce, mustard, salt and pepper. Mix well. Divide and mould into 4 burger shapes. Place on plates and garnish with anchovy. Serve with salad.

Serves 4

STEAK PHYLLIS

A version of Steak Diane, named after the cook, *Jim Bowen*'s wife – Phyllis!

4 oz/100 g butter
1 onion, peeled and chopped
4 × 6 oz/175 g fillet steaks, beaten thin
juice and grated rind of ½ lemon
dash of Worcestershire sauce
salt and pepper
1 tbsp parsley, chopped
2 tbsp brandy, warmed
2 tbsp double cream

Melt half the butter in a frying pan and fry onion until soft. Remove with a slotted spoon. Add remaining butter to pan and quickly fry steaks over a high heat. Remove and keep warm. Return onion to pan, stir in lemon juice and rind, Worcestershire sauce, and season with salt and pepper. Add parsley and brandy, and ignite. When the flames have disappeared, stir cream into sauce and pour over steaks.

Serves 4

BOEUF EN CROÛTE

Fillets of beef wrapped in pastry.

1 onion, peeled and chopped
1 oz/25 g butter
4 oz/100 g mushrooms, wiped and chopped
½ tsp fresh thyme, chopped
salt and pepper
4 × 6 oz/175 g fillet steaks
13 oz/375 g packet frozen puff pastry, defrosted
1 egg, beaten

Fry onion in butter until soft. Add mushrooms and fry for 2 minutes. Season with thyme, salt and pepper. Cool. Brown steaks quickly in a little oil. Cool. Roll pastry thinly and cut into 4 neat squares. Place steaks in each square. Spoon onion and mushroom mixture over each. Wrap up pastry to make a parcel, dampening edges to seal. Place on a lightly oiled tray, brush with beaten egg and bake at Gas 7/425°/220°C for 20 minutes or until golden brown.

Serves 4

DAME EDNA'S SADDLE OF DINGO

When cooking, Dame Edna always wears rubber gloves – not for protection but as a fashion statement.

Dame Edna always says 'when available' after her ingredients, so when dingo is in short supply, use lamb instead.

1 prepared saddle of lamb
2 tbsp oil
salt and pepper
watercress to garnish

Place saddle of lamb in a large roasting tin. Brush with oil, season, and roast in a hot oven at Gas 5/275°F/190°C, allowing 20 minutes per lb plus 20 minutes, or until golden and juices run pink. To serve, cut thick, wedge-shaped slices from each side, parallel to the backbone. Garnish.

Serves 4-6

BANNER HEADLINE

These hot and spicy meatballs are just like *Derek Jameson*'s taste in newspaper stories.

1 small onion, peeled and chopped
1 clove garlic, crushed
2 tbsp oil
15 oz/425 g tin chopped tomatoes
salt and freshly ground black pepper

Meatballs
1 small onion, peeled and finely chopped
1 lb/450 g minced lamb
1 tsp cumin seeds
1 tsp cayenne pepper
salt and freshly ground black pepper
1 egg, beaten

For the sauce, fry onion and garlic in oil. Add tomatoes and season with salt and pepper. Bring to the boil and simmer for 15 minutes.

For the meatballs, mix all ingredients together and form into balls on a lightly floured surface. Fry in a little oil until browned and cooked through. Drain on kitchen paper.

Purée sauce until smooth and serve with meatballs on a bed of cooked rice.

Serves 4

GOOD SHEPHERD'S PIE

Playing a parson in the TV series 'All in Good Faith', *Richard Briers* found this a filling and interesting variation of the traditional dish.

1 large onion, peeled and sliced
1 oz/25 g butter
1½ lb/675 g minced cooked pork and stuffing
½ small Bramley apple, peeled, cored and grated
dash Worcestershire sauce
½ pint/300 ml chicken stock
1 tsp yeast extract
salt and pepper
2 tsp flour mixed in 1tbsp water
1 lb/450 g left-over cooked potatoes and carrots

Fry onion in butter until soft. Add pork and stuffing, apple and Worcestershire sauce. Pour over stock, add yeast extract and season with salt and pepper. Bring to boil and simmer for 10 minutes. Add flour paste. Heat until sauce thickens. Put mince in ovenproof dish. Mash together potato and carrot, and pipe rosettes over meat. Bake at Gas 6/400°F/200°C for 25-30 minutes until golden on top.

Serves 4

Richard Briers enjoys a forkful of Good Shepherd's Pie.

BEEF STROGANOFF

Fast skillet dish of strips of rump steak in a delicious mustard and soured cream sauce from the kitchen of Jim Bowen.

1 onion, peeled and sliced
8 oz/225 g mushrooms, wiped and sliced
2 oz/50 g butter
2 tsp made mustard
1 tbsp oil
1 lb/450 g rump steak, cut into strips
¼ pint/150 ml soured cream
salt and pepper
watercress to garnish

Fry onion and mushrooms in butter until soft and stir in mustard. Remove with a slotted spoon and add oil to pan. Fry steak quickly and return mushrooms and onions to pan. Stir in soured cream and season with salt and pepper. Gently heat through. Place on a heated serving dish, garnish with watercress and serve with boiled rice.

Serves 4

Three tasty slow cook dishes from *Trudie Goodwin* alias WPc June Ackland of ITV's 'The Bill'.

HANDCUFFS

Pork chops with prunes cooked slowly in cider and finished with cream.

2 oz/50 g butter
1 large onion, peeled and chopped
1 tbsp chives, chopped
4 large loin pork chops, trimmed
seasoned flour
½ pint/300 ml dry cider
8 prunes, stoned
4 tbsp double cream
salt and ground black pepper

Melt butter in a pan, add onion and chives, and fry until onion is soft. Toss chops in flour, add to pan and cook both sides until browned. Place in an ovenproof dish and pour over cider. Add prunes, cover and cook at Gas 2/300°F/150°C for 3-5 hours. Remove, and stir in cream and seasoning before serving.

Serves 4

ON THE BEAT

Half leg of lamb cooked slowly with apricots. After a few hours, the sweetness blends with the lamb juices for a delicious sauce.

2 tbsp oil
½ leg of lamb
seasoned flour
1 onion, peeled and chopped
2 cloves garlic, peeled and crushed
1 tbsp ground coriander
15 oz/425 g tin apricot halves in syrup
salt and black pepper

Heat oil in a large flameproof casserole with a lid. Coat lamb in seasoned flour and cook in oil until lightly browned. Remove and keep to one side. Add onion, garlic and coriander, and stir for 3-4 minutes. Place lamb on top, pour over apricots and juice, cover and cook at Gas 2/300°F/150°C for 4-6 hours, or until tender.

Serves 4

ROZZERS

2 tbsp olive oil
1½ lb/700 g stewing steak, trimmed and cut into chunks
seasoned flour
2 onions, peeled and sliced into rings
2 cloves garlic, crushed
¼ pint/150 ml red wine
½ pint/300 ml beef stock
4 oz/100 g button mushrooms, quartered
1 onion, peeled and stuck with 3 cloves
2 bay leaves
sprig of thyme
salt and ground black pepper

Heat oil in a large frying pan. Toss steak in seasoned flour and add to pan. Brown all over, remove with a slotted spoon and place in an ovenproof casserole. Fry onions and garlic for 5 minutes. Remove and add to casserole. Pour over wine and stock, and add mushrooms, onion with cloves, bay leaves, thyme, salt and pepper. Cover and cook at Gas 2/300°F/150°F for 4-6 hours, or until beef is tender.

Serves 4

WPc June Ackland alias Trudie Goodwin looks forward to a dish like On the Beat for dinner – slow-cooked meals suit the lifestyles of both a WPc and an actress.

STAN DOES HIS WURST!

Liverpool comic *Stan Boardman* recalls, 'After the Germans bombed our chip shop, we had to live on sausages . . . sausages and Heinz beans – the German ones! The Germans love food,' he maintains. 'That's why they named all their cities after it . . . Frankfurt . . . Hamburg.'

In spite of Stan's jokes at the expense of the German nation, he owns a Mercedes car and his dog is a German shepherd, named Rosco, who obligingly eats the scouse when Stan burns it. Scouse is a traditional Liverpool dish and one of Stan's specialities, which he makes with left-over meat from one of his wife Vivienne's delicious Sunday lunches. The scouse – and the lunches – are rare treats for him since he travels so much in his work.

Sausages, however, remain a favourite; sausage and mash, toad-in-the-hole, and sausage, chips and beans, all have nostalgic appeal. As Stan says, sausages are so friendly – they're always linked together. But here's a string of unusual sausage dishes that also get his seal of approval.

PIZZA POLANA

Spicy tomato and salami slices on a pizza base.

Pizza base
1 tsp sugar
¼ pint/150 ml tepid water
1 tsp dried yeast
8 oz/225 g strong plain flour
½ tsp salt
½ oz/15 g butter

Topping
1 onion, peeled and finely chopped
½ oz/15 g butter
14 oz/400 g tin tomatoes, chopped and drained
salt and ground black pepper
8 slices salami
1 black olive

For the base, dissolve sugar in water. Sprinkle yeast over the water and leave in a warm place for 10 minutes or until frothy. Sift flour and salt into a bowl, rub in butter, and pour in yeast liquid. Mix to a soft dough. Knead for 10 minutes on lightly floured surface. Place in oiled polythene bag and leave in a warm place until doubled in size. Grease an 8 in/20 cm flan ring on a baking sheet. Line the flan ring with dough. Leave in a warm place.

For the topping, fry the onion in butter until soft. Add tomatoes, remove from heat and season. Spread over pizza base, arrange salami on top, place olive in centre and cook at Gas 7/425°F/220°C for 20-25 minutes.

Serves 4

GRETEL'S PROMISE

Filling salad with chopped frankfurters.

2 lb/900 g potatoes, peeled, cooked and cut into chunks
4 frankfurters, sliced
1 bunch spring onions, trimmed and chopped
4 gherkins, sliced
3 tbsp soured cream
1 tsp horseradish sauce
salt and pepper

Mix together the potatoes, frankfurters, spring onions and gherkins. Blend soured cream, horseradish sauce, salt and pepper and stir. Mix with potatoes and frankfurters.

Serves 4

Let loose in a German-sausage factory, Stan Boardman is in his element.

FRAÜLEIN'S FANCY

Herby sausage filling in a puff pastry plait.

1 small onion, peeled and chopped
½ oz/15 g butter
4 oz/100 g button mushrooms, chopped
1 lb/450 g sausagemeat
1 tsp dried sage
salt and pepper
13 oz/375 g packet frozen puff pastry, thawed
1 egg, beaten

Fry onion in butter until soft. Add mushrooms and fry for 2 minutes. Drain, add to sausagemeat with sage, and season.

Roll out pastry into a large rectangle. Trim the edges. Place sausage stuffing down the middle, lengthways. Make diagonal cuts, about 1 in/2.5 cm apart, down both long edges. Fold strips from alternate sides over stuffing to cover and to form plait. Seal with water. Place on lightly-greased baking sheet, brush with egg and cook at Gas 7/ 425°F/220°C for 30-35 minutes or until golden. Serve sliced, hot or cold.

Serves 4-6

CHIP SHOP CHARLIES

Savoury saveloys with old-fashioned pease pudding.

1 lb/450 g dried yellow split peas, soaked overnight
2 oz/50 g butter
1 egg, beaten
salt and pepper
pinch nutmeg
4 saveloys

Drain peas and place in a large pan. Cover with water, bring to boil and simmer for 1 hour or until tender. Drain and mash with a fork. Stir in butter, egg, salt, pepper and nutmeg. Butter a pudding basin and spoon in mixture. Cover with foil and steam for 1 hour until pudding is firm.

Cover saveloys with boiling water and stand for 4 minutes to heat through. Drain and serve with pudding.

Serves 4

PORKENAPPLEN

German casserole of sausages with apples.

1½ lb/700 g pork sausages
1 tbsp oil
1 large onion, peeled and cut into rings
½ pint/300 ml beer
1 apple, cored and cut into chunks
salt and pepper
sliced apple to garnish

Fry sausages in oil until browned on all sides and cooked through. Remove and add onion to pan and cook until soft. Return sausages, pour in beer and add the apple. Season with salt and pepper. Simmer for 20 minutes. Garnish with apple slices.

Serves 4

CHICO

Chicken flavoured with spicy Spanish sausage.

1 onion, peeled and sliced
1 clove garlic, crushed
1 tbsp oil
4 chicken breasts, skinned, boned and cut into chunks
½ oz/15 g flour
¾ pint/425 ml chicken stock
salt and pepper
4 oz/100 g black olives
1 red pepper, seeded and cut into rings
6 tomatoes, peeled and quartered
4 oz/100 g chorizo sausage, thinly sliced
chopped parsley

Fry onion and garlic in oil until soft. Add chicken and fry for 5 minutes. Stir in flour and stock. Bring to the boil and simmer for 30 minutes. Season. Add olives, pepper, tomatoes and sausage, and simmer for 15 minutes. Serve garnished with parsley.

Serves 4

Spice 'n' Rice

In his bachelor days TV-am's early-bird presenter, *Mike Morris*, was a confirmed beer and curry man. 'I wasn't a very adventurous curry eater though,' he confesses. 'I'd stick with the same dish for a couple of years, then change to the next one.'
These days he usually chooses mildly-spiced curries rather than the hot ones he used to go for, and is experimenting with cooking his own: 'I love Indian food so much, I can see it might become an obsession, grinding my own spices, and buying special ingredients. I hate admitting failure – and any curry I made would have to be just perfect! There was a time when it was a test of virility to eat the tonsil-scorchers!' But these days, he's keeping cool.

Lamb Pasanda

Mildly-spiced lamb in an almond and cream sauce.

1 large onion, peeled and sliced
2 cloves garlic, crushed
2 tbsp oil
2 tsp garam masala
1 in/2 cm piece root ginger
few cloves
black peppercorns
5 cardamon pods
½ tsp chilli powder
½ tsp turmeric
1 bay leaf
½ stick cinnamon
1 oz/25 g ground almonds
½ tsp salt
1½ lb/700 g leg of lamb, fat trimmed and cut into strips
½ pint/300 ml water
2 tbsp cream

Fry onion and garlic in oil until soft. Stir in all spices, herbs, almonds and salt and cook for 1 minute. Add lamb and fry until brown. Add water, bring to boil, simmer and cook uncovered for 1 hour adding extra liquid if necessary. Stir in cream and gently reheat. Serve with rice and poppadums.

Serves 4

Prawn Maharaja

Luxury curry using king prawns. Small prawns can be substituted.

1 onion, peeled and sliced
2 cloves garlic, crushed
2 tbsp oil
½ tsp ginger root, chopped
1 tsp turmeric
2 tsp garam masala
1 tsp ground coriander
1 bay leaf
1 cinnamon stick
few black peppercorns
1 tsp salt
6 tomatoes, peeled and chopped
8 oz/225 g prawns, peeled
2 tbsp cream
few coriander leaves to garnish

Fry onion and garlic in oil until soft. Add all the spices and stir for 2 minutes. Add tomatoes and heat gently for 10 minutes. Stir in prawns and cream and heat through. Garnish with coriander.

Serves 4

PILAU RICE

Spicy dry rice.

8 oz/225 g basmati rice
2 oz/50 g butter
6 cloves
1 cinnamon stick
1 tsp black peppercorns
1 tsp cumin seeds
½ tsp salt
1 pint/600 ml water

Wash rice in cold water and drain. Melt butter in large pan and fry cloves, cinnamon, peppercorns, cumin and salt for 2 minutes. Reduce heat, add rice and water. Cook gently for about 12 minutes. Drain excess liquid, and cover in ovenproof dish. Cook at Gas 5/375°F/190°C for 10 minutes. Fluff up with fork.

Serves 4

POPPADUMS

Crispy thin pancakes, available at supermarkets.

Grill until poppadums swell and bubble. Serve cool and crisp.

ONION AND CUCUMBER RAITA

Cooling yoghurt and mint dip, flavoured with garlic.

½ cucumber, finely chopped
½ tsp salt
¼ pint/150 ml natural yoghurt
½ tsp white wine vinegar
1 clove garlic, crushed
½ onion, peeled and finely chopped
1 tbsp mint, chopped

Sprinkle cucumber with salt and leave for 15 minutes. Rinse and drain. Add yoghurt, vinegar, garlic onion and mix together. Spoon into a serving dish and top with mint.

Serves 4

LADIES' TALONS

Okra in a lightly spiced green chilli sauce.

1 lb/450 g okra, wiped
1 onion, peeled and chopped
1 clove garlic, crushed
2 oz/50 g butter
7 oz/200 g tin tomatoes, chopped
1 green chilli, finely chopped
½ tsp cumin seeds
½ tsp ground coriander
1 tsp garam masala
1 tbsp lemon juice
salt and pepper

Top and tail okra. Fry onion and garlic in butter until soft. Add tomatoes, okra, and remaining ingredients, and cook for 10 minutes.

Serves 4

BEEF AND SPINACH CURRY

1 onion, sliced
2 cloves garlic, crushed
2 oz/50 g butter
1 bay leaf
1 cinnamon stick
few whole cloves
few cardamon pods
1 in/2 cm piece root ginger, chopped
1 tsp tumeric
2 tsp chilli powder
2 tsp garam masala
1 lb/450 g stewing steak, trimmed and cubed
14 oz/425 g tin tomatoes, chopped
salt
¼ pint/150 ml water
2 oz/50 g frozen whole leaf spinach, thawed

Fry onion and garlic cloves in butter. Add all spices and cook for 2 minutes. Add meat and fry until browned. Pour over tomatoes and season. Add water then cover and cook for 1½ hours or until meat is tender. Stir in spinach 10 minutes before end of cooking time.

Serves 4

TANDOORI CHICKEN

Gently spiced chicken portions served with salad and ONION AND CUCUMBER RAITA.

3 lb/1.4 kg chicken, jointed
½ pint/300 ml natural yoghurt
juice of ½ lemon
salt and pepper
2 tbsp tandoori curry powder
1 large clove garlic, crushed
1 lettuce, shredded
1 lime, cut into wedges

Wash and wipe chicken, and place in a large bowl. Mix yoghurt, lemon juice, salt, pepper, tandoori powder, and garlic. Pour over chicken and leave to marinate in fridge overnight. Place under a hot grill until cooked through. Serve on a bed of lettuce and decorate with lime wedges. Also serve with a refreshing side dish of Onion and Cucumber Raita, as a tasty dip.

Serves 4

Vegetables and Salads

Best-quality vegetables should be crisp, fresh and brightly coloured. Choose from the international selection available in greengrocers and supermarkets for healthy, vitamin-packed dishes. Try to serve a main vegetable dish at least once a week: it's good for you – and much cheaper than meat.

There are surprises galore when *Cilla Black* cooks up dinner.

GOSH! POTS

Red peppers surprisingly filled with a crunchy, healthy salad of fruit, nuts and vegetables topped with fetta cheese cubes and dressed with Greek yoghurt.

4 red peppers
4 oz/100 g grapes, halved
2 sticks celery, chopped
2 carrots, peeled and cut into strips
2 oz/50 g black olives
2 oz/50 g flaked almonds
4 tbsp Greek yoghurt
2 oz/50 g fetta cheese, cut into small cubes

Slice tops from peppers, and keep. Remove seeds inside. Blanch in boiling water for 2 minutes, plunge in cold water, drain and dry.

In a bowl mix together grapes, celery, carrots, olives and almonds with yoghurt. Spoon into peppers and top with fetta cheese. Replace tops as lids.

Serves 4

HIDDEN TREASURE

Jacket potatoes, scooped out to bury the golden treasure of crispy bacon and a poached egg.

4 large baking potatoes, scrubbed
4 slices streaky bacon, de-rinded and chopped
1 oz/25 g butter
salt and pepper
4 eggs

Score potatoes, wrap in foil and put on a baking tray. Cook at Gas 6/400°F/200°C for 1 hour or until soft. Fry bacon in butter until crisp. Fold back foil and scoop out enough potato to accommodate bacon and egg. Spoon bacon into cavities in potatoes and season with salt and pepper. Crack an egg into each potato and re-seal foil. Return to oven for 5 minutes or until egg has set.

Serves 4

BEADLE'S FRUIT SALAD

This mixed fruit salad with a French dressing is not a *Jeremy Beadle* joke. It is in fact delicious served as an accompaniment to cold meat.

3 kiwi fruit, peeled and sliced
3 pears, peeled, cored and sliced lengthways
2 oranges, peeled and segmented
1 pineapple, skinned, eyes removed and sliced
1 small bunch seedless white grapes
12 dates, halved and stoned
2 apples, cored and cut into chunks
1 pink grapefruit, peeled and segmented
1 melon, cut in half and scooped out with melon baller
1 mango, peeled and sliced

Salad dressing
6 tbsp olive oil
juice of 1 lemon
few mint leaves, chopped
1 tbsp parsley, chopped

Put all the fruit in a large glass bowl. Mix oil and lemon juice and pour over dressing. Chill before serving. Decorate with mint and parsley.

Serves 6

Cilla Black takes the lid off a red pepper and its 'Surprise, Surprise!'

BROCCOLI QUICHE

Good filling fare from actress *Ann Beach*.

10 oz/275 g plain flour
½ tsp salt
2½ oz/65 g lard
2½ oz/65 g margarine
approx. 5 tbsp cold water
12 oz/350 g broccoli, trimmed, blanched and chopped
4 oz/100 g Cheddar cheese, grated
½ pint/300 ml milk
2 eggs
salt and pepper

Sift flour and salt into a bowl. Rub in fat until breadcrumb stage. Make a well in the centre and add water. Mix with a knife until it forms a dough. Turn out onto floured board, and knead for 2 minutes. Wrap and chill for 30 minutes.

Roll pastry out to fit a 12 in/30 cm lightly-oiled, loose-bottomed quiche tin. Trim edges, and leave to rest for 30 minutes. Bake pastry case blind for 20 minutes at Gas 6/400°F/200°C. Remove and leave to cool.

Place broccoli in bottom of pastry case. Sprinkle over cheese. Beat milk, eggs, salt and pepper together and pour over broccoli. Bake at Gas 4/350°F/180°C for 40 minutes or until set and lightly browned.

Eat hot or cold, garnished with tomato.

Serves 8

INDIAN SUMMER

Actress *Angela Thorne* enjoys this sultry mix of raw cauliflower, celery, apples and cashew nuts in a light curry sauce.

1 large cauliflower, divided into florets, washed and
   dried
4 sticks celery, sliced
4 oz/100 g cashew nuts
2 red apples, cored and chopped
¼ pint/150 ml mayonnaise
1 tsp curry powder
salt and pepper

Mix together cauliflower, celery, nuts and apple in a bowl. Mix mayonnaise, curry powder, salt and pepper and stir together.

Serves 6

Jill Gascoine's Vegetable Stew.

A vegetarian diet suits *Jill Gascoine*, and her ideas are unusual and tasty.

MUSHROOMS WITH SAGE

Hot first course or supper dish of mushrooms fried gently in butter with sage and fresh Parmesan, for the best flavour.

3 oz/75 g butter
1 lb/450 g button mushrooms, wiped
4 tbsp fresh Parmesan cheese, grated
1 tbsp sage, chopped
salt and pepper
fresh sage leaves to decorate

Melt butter in a large frying pan. Add mushrooms and quickly fry for 3 minutes, stirring as they cook. Add Parmesan, sage, salt and pepper, and stir through, cooking until cheese melts. Decorate with sage leaves.

Serves 4

VEGETABLE STEW

With a tasty peanut sauce.

1 onion, cut into rings
4 tbsp oil
2 carrots, cut in strips
1 parsnip, peeled and sliced
1 turnip, peeled and cubed
½ celeriac, peeled and cubed
1 pint/600 ml vegetable stock
few sprigs thyme
salt and pepper
4 oz/100 g green beans, topped and tailed
4 courgettes, thickly sliced
2 leeks, washed and sliced
2 tbsp smooth peanut butter
4 oz/100 g Cheddar cheese, grated

Fry onion in oil until soft. Add carrots, parsnips, turnip and celeriac, and fry for a few minutes more. Add stock, thyme, salt and pepper. Bring to the boil and simmer for 8 minutes. Add beans, courgettes, leeks and simmer for a further 5 minutes.
　　Mix peanut butter with 4 tbsp cooking liquid. Stir into stew with cheese.

Serves 4

Roy Walker, the Irish comedian and quiz show host, is mad about potatoes, which is not surprising since he was brought up on them.

FADGE

Triangular potato cakes, usually served with bacon and eggs for breakfast.

1 oz/25 g butter, melted
1 lb/450 g mashed potatoes
2 tbsp plain flour
salt

Mix butter into potatoes. Mix in flour and salt, to make a stiff, dough-like paste. Roll out on floured top to ½ in/1 cm thick. Cut into 4 triangles. Lightly grease a griddle or frying pan. Fry for 3 minutes each side.

Serves 4

COLCANNON

Traditional Irish potato and cabbage recipe, piled in a serving dish with melted butter poured into a well in the centre.

1 lb/450 g green cabbage
1 bunch spring onions, chopped
¼ pint/150 ml milk
2 lb/900 g boiled potatoes, peeled and cut into even pieces
pinch nutmeg
salt and pepper
2 oz/50 g butter, melted

Cook cabbage in boiling salted water. Drain and chop. Cook spring onions in milk until soft. Mash potato and add milk and onion mixture. Stir in cabbage, nutmeg and seasoning. Pile into heated serving dish and pour melted butter into a well in the centre.

Serves 4

LUCK OF THE IRISH

Fat and flat omelette filled with potato. Serve hot or cold, cut into wedges like a cake.

1 medium onion, peeled and chopped
2 tbsp oil
1 lb/450 g potatoes, diced, boiled
8 eggs
3 tbsp water
salt and pepper

Fry onion until soft in oil in a large frying pan. Add potatoes and heat through. Beat eggs, water and seasoning together and pour over. Cook over low heat until egg begins to set. Loosen edges with knife. Place under hot grill to finish cooking top. Turn out, cut into wedges.

Serves 4

MURPHYS

Potatoes in their jackets, stuffed with crisp bacon and topped with grated cheese.

4 baking potatoes
1 oz/25 g butter
4 oz/100 g Cheddar cheese, grated
1 egg yolk
salt and pepper
4 rashers streaky bacon, derinded and chopped

Cut slits across each potato and bake for 1 hour at Gas 6/400°F/200°C, or until cooked through.

Scoop out middle, leaving skin as a shell. Mix potatoes with butter, half cheese, egg yolk, salt and pepper. Fry bacon until crisp and spoon into potato shells. Fit piping bag with large star nozzle and fill skins with potato mixture. Top with remaining cheese and reheat in oven for 10 minutes until cheese melts.

Serves 4

LEPRECHAUN'S REVENGE

Layered potato cake with red and green peppers, onions, cheese, milk, cream and eggs.

1 lb/450 g potatoes, peeled, sliced
1 red pepper, de-seeded and cut into rings
1 green pepper, de-seeded and cut into rings
1 onion, peeled and cut into rings
1 tbsp oil
4 oz/100 g Cheddar cheese, grated
½ pint/300 ml milk
¼ pint/150 ml single cream
3 eggs
salt and pepper

Line a 6 in/15 cm soufflé dish with greased foil. Blanch potatoes in boiling salted water for 6-8 minutes until just soft. Blanch peppers in boiling salted water for 2-3 minutes. Fry onion in oil until soft. Layer potatoes, peppers, onion and cheese, leaving some for top. Finish with potato layer. Sprinkle over remaining cheese. Beat together milk, cream, eggs and seasoning. Pour over potatoes. Cook for 1 hour at Gas 4/350°F/180°C or until set. Cool, take out of dish and remove foil. Serve in slices.

Serves 6

Punch-ups from Hale and Pace.

PUNCH UPS

Hale and Pace go for the mixed vegetable patties which are rather like bubble and squeak burgers.

1 small onion, peeled and chopped
1 oz/25 g butter
2 lb/900 g potatoes, peeled, chopped and cooked
1 lb/450 g green cabbage, shredded and cooked
1 egg, beaten
salt and fresh ground black pepper
flour for coating

Fry onion in butter until soft. Put potatoes, cabbage and onion in a large bowl. Stir in egg and season with salt and pepper. Form into burger shapes and coat in flour. Fry both sides in a little oil until browned.

Serves 4

COURGETTE AND CARROT RIBBONS

This pretty salad of thin raw strips of courgette and carrot curled into ribbons and served with a lemon dressing suits *Bruce Forsyth* down to the ground.

2 lb/900 g carrots, scraped
2 lb/900 g courgettes, trimmed

Lemon dressing
6 tbsp olive oil
3 tbsp fresh squeezed lemon juice
1tsp mustard
salt and fresh ground black pepper

Thinly pare strips from carrots and courgettes with a potato peeler. Place them in ice-cold water and leave until curled slightly. Drain. Arrange vegetables in a serving dish.

Shake all dressing ingredients together in a screw-top jar and pour over before serving.

Serves 4

RUMBLE DE THUMPS

North of the border bubble-and-squeak from *Siobhan Redmond*. It can be served as a side dish – or make a lot for a main meal.

1 oz/25 g butter
1 medium onion, peeled and chopped
1 lb/450 g mashed potatoes
1 lb/450 g cooked cabbage
2 oz/50 g cheese, grated
1 tbsp choppped chives

Melt butter and gently cook onion until soft but not brown. Add potatoes and cabbage. Season. Pile into buttered pie dish and sprinkle the cheese over it. Brown under a hot grill. Sprinkle chives over the top before serving.

Serves 4

Food of the vegetable variety features frequently on the menu of *Jon* and *Ingeborg Pertwee*. This is not so surprising, since Jon's other persona is Worzel Gummidge, the loveable scarecrow.

VEGETABLE PATCHWORK

Pretty, striped terrine of carrots, spinach, cauliflower and French beans wrapped in lettuce.

3 large lettuce leaves, blanched
1 lb/450 g carrots, cooked
2 whole eggs
salt and pepper
1 small onion, grated
3 egg whites
8 oz/225 g chopped frozen spinach, defrosted
1 clove garlic, crushed
½ tsp ground nutmeg
1 small cauliflower in florets, cooked
1 tbsp grated Parmesan cheese
2 oz/50 g thin French beans, blanched

Line a 1 lb/450 g oiled loaf tin with lettuce leaves. Purée carrots with eggs, salt, pepper and grated onion, and pour half into the tin. Beat 2 egg whites stiff. Fold into the spinach with garlic, nutmeg, salt and pepper. Pour half the mix over carrot. Purée cauliflower with Parmesan cheese. Beat remaining egg white stiff and fold in. Pour half over spinach, lay green beans on top, and cover with remaining cauliflower mixture. Finish with another spinach, then carrot layer. Cook in a water-bath (*bain-marie*) at Gas 4/350°F/180°C for 35-40 minutes. Cool, than turn out. Slice and serve with red pepper sauce.

Serves 4

RED PEPPER SAUCE

½ onion, peeled and chopped
1 red pepper, de-seeded and chopped
2 tbsp oil
¼ pint/150 ml chicken stock
salt and pepper

Cook onion and pepper in oil until soft. Add stock. Simmer for 10 minutes. Purée. Return to a clean pan, reheat to reduce slightly. Season. Chill before serving.

AUNT SALLY COLLY

Cauliflower with egg and breadcrumb garnish.

1 small cauliflower, trimmed and left whole
2 hard-boiled eggs, shelled
1 tbsp parsley, chopped
4 oz/100 g butter
2 oz/50 g fresh breadcrumbs

Cook cauliflower in boiling salted water for 8 minutes, and drain. Place on warmed serving dish. Remove yolks from egg whites. Chop whites finely and sieve yolk. Mix egg white with parsley and arrange around cauliflower. Melt butter in a pan, add breadcrumbs and cook for 2 minutes. Pour over cauliflower and decorate top with sieved egg yolk.

Serves 4

PERTWEE'S PLATTER

A colourful way of presenting vegetables.

2 parsnips, peeled and quartered
1 lb/450 g broccoli, cut into florets
1 lb/450 g new potatoes, scrubbed
2 corn on the cob, trimmed and cut into 2 in/5 cm slices
8 oz/225 g French green beans, topped and tailed
1 lb/450 g asparagus, stalks trimmed

Cook each vegetable separately in boiling salted water until just cooked. Drain. Arrange in a pattern on a large serving platter.

Serves 4

SCARECROW'S SURPRISE

Fennel in tomato sauce. Serve hot as a vegetable dish or cold as a salad.

2 fennel, trimmed and quartered
1 small onion, peeled and chopped
1 clove garlic, crushed
1 tbsp oil
15 oz/425 g can tomatoes, chopped
salt and pepper
few basil leaves for decoration

Cook fennel in boiling salted water for 6 minutes. Cook onion and garlic in oil until soft. Add tomatoes, salt and pepper. Simmer for 10 minutes. Purée in liquidiser, return to clean pan and reheat.
Place the fennel on a serving dish, pour over tomato sauce and decorate with basil leaves.

COUNTRY DIP AND VEGETABLES

Raw crunch with a delicious creamy dip.

½ pint/300 ml soured cream
2 tbsp creamed horseradish
salt and pepper
1 tbsp chopped chives
½ onion, peeled and chopped
cucumber, celery, carrot, red pepper and green pepper cut into sticks

Mix together cream, horseradish and seasoning until blended. Stir in some of the chives, and onion. Garnish with more chives. Serve with vegetable sticks.

WORZEL PIE

Tasty potato dish.

1 clove garlic, finely chopped
3 tbsp oil
3 lb/1.4 kg potatoes, peeled and thinly sliced
1 onion, peeled and sliced
salt and pepper
½ pint/300 ml chicken stock
2 oz/50 g butter

Gently fry garlic in 1 tbsp of the oil and sprinkle in the base of an ovenproof dish. Cook the potatoes in boiling salted water for 4 minutes, drain. Fry the sliced onions in the remaining oil slowly until softened.
Put alternate layers of potatoes and onions in dish, sprinkling each with salt and pepper. Pour over stock, dot top with butter and cook at Gas 6/ 400°F/200°C for about 45 minutes or until potatoes are cooked when tested with a knife and top is browned.

Serves 4

Bruce Forsyth's Courgette and Carrot Ribbons (see page 63).

CUCUMBER SALAD WITH MINT

Crisp and refreshing salad of wafer-thin cucumber slices in a minty, soured cream dressing.

1 cucumber
1 tsp salt

Soured cream dressing
¼ pint/150 ml soured cream
2 tbsp olive oil
salt and pepper
1 tbsp fresh mint, chopped
1 sprig mint for decoration

Cut cucumber into thin slices. Put in a colander and sprinkle over salt. Leave for 30 minutes for excess water to drain away. Wash under cold water to rinse away salt. Drain. Mix soured cream, oil, salt, pepper and chopped mint. Add cucumber and stir until well-coated. Arrange in serving dish and decorate with sprig of mint.

Serves 4

BEANS AND MUSHROOM SALAD

Vegetables in a light yoghurt mayonnaise.

10 oz/275 g can broad beans, drained or 10 oz/275 g
    cooked broad beans
8 oz/225 g French beans, topped, tailed and blanched
4 oz/100 g button mushrooms, wiped.

Mayonnaise
1 egg yolk
½ tsp made mustard
1 tsp vinegar
salt and pepper
¼ pint/150 ml sunflower oil
2 tbsp natural yoghurt

Mix beans and mushrooms in a bowl. For mayonnaise, whisk yolk with mustard, vinegar, salt and pepper. Gradually whisk in oil drip by drip until beginning to thicken. Then add in a thin stream until mix is thick and creamy. Stir in yoghurt. Spoon through beans mixture.

Serves 4

HOME-MADE BAKED BEANS

Trudie Goodwin likes to eat vegetarian when she can. These baked beans are the absolutely irresistible home-made variety. The recipe contains bacon, but leave this out for complete vegetarians.

1 red pepper, seeded and chopped
1 onion, peeled and finely chopped
2 rashers bacon, de-rinded and chopped (optional)
1 tbsp oil
8 oz/225 g haricot beans, soaked overnight
14 oz/400 g tin tomatoes, chopped
1 tbsp Worcestershire sauce
1 tbsp English mustard
1 tbsp brown sugar
ground black pepper

Fry pepper, onion and bacon in oil for 4 minutes. Place in a pan with remaining ingredients and stir well. Bring to a rolling boil for 10 minutes. Pour into an ovenproof casserole, cover and cook for 8-10 hours at Gas 2/300°F/150°C, topping up with water, if necessary.

Serves 4

CRUNCHY SALAD

A lovely mix of crunchy fruit and vegetables in a savoury French dressing from *Angela Thorne*.

1 lb/450 g carrots, peeled and grated
1 celeriac, peeled and grated
½ fresh pineapple, peeled and cut into strips

French dressing
2 tbsp white wine vinegar
6 tbsp olive oil
½ tbsp mustard
1 tbsp basil, chopped
salt and pepper

Mix carrots, celeriac and pineapple in a large bowl.
   For the dressing, mix the white wine vinegar, olive oil, mustard, chopped basil and seasoning together, and pour over the prepared salad.

Serves 6

Slender as a French bean and graceful as a gazelle, *Grace Kennedy* attributes her shape to a love of healthy salads such as the following.

GERMAN POTATO SALAD WITH FRANKFURTERS

Scrumptious new potato salad with sliced frankfurters in a herby vinaigrette. Use firm fleshed Maris Piper or small Cyprus Nicola potatoes.

2 lb/900 g small potatoes
2 frankfurters, sliced

Chive dressing
2 tbsp garlic vinegar
½ tsp made mustard
salt and pepper
6 tbsp olive oil
1 tbsp chives, chopped

Scrub potatoes, leaving skins on. Cook in a pan of boiling salted water until tender. Drain and cool. Mix with frankfurters and arrange in a serving dish. Put vinegar, mustard, salt, pepper, oil and chives in a screw-top jar. Shake well to blend. Pour over potato salad.

Serves 4

HOT POTATO SALAD WITH CHIVES

Delicious chives added to hot potato salad. Use waxy potatoes for the best texture.

1½ lb/700 g new potatoes
¼ pint/150 ml soured cream
grated rind and juice of ½ lemon
salt and pepper
4 tbsp chopped chives

Scrub potatoes. Cook in boiling salted water for 15 minutes or until just tender. Mix soured cream with lemon juice and rind. Season with salt and pepper and stir in chives. Drain potatoes, and stir in soured cream to coat.

Jon and Ingeborg Pertwee sampling the fresh-cooked garden vegetables from Pertwee's Platter (see page 64).

Enthusiastic gardener Jill Gascoine likes to add herbs to her vegetarian dishes for subtle flavourings (for mint drink, see page 115)

CHICORY, ORANGE AND WALNUT SALAD

Refreshing mix of bitter chicory, sweet orange slices and nuts in a lemon French dressing.

2 heads chicory, leaves separated, washed and dried
4 oranges, peeled, pith removed and cut into slices
2 oz/50 g walnut halves

Lemon dressing
4 tbsp sunflower or walnut oil
1 tbsp lemon juice
1 tbsp Dijon mustard
1 tbsp fresh chopped oregano or parsley

Arrange chicory leaves around the edge of a serving dish. Place orange slices in the centre and top with walnuts. Shake dressing ingredients together in a screw-top jar. Pour over salad just before serving.

Serves 4

TIMSON BROWN RICE SALAD

A filling and healthy brown rice salad studded with corn, mushrooms, nuts and raisins makes a good after theatre snack for *Penelope Keith*. Timson is husband Roddy's name.

8 oz/225 g brown rice
6 oz/175 g can sweet corn, drained
2 oz/50 g button mushrooms, wiped and sliced
2 oz/50 g raisins
3 oz/75 g cashew nuts
salt and pepper

Salad dressing
1 tbsp white wine vinegar
2 tbsp olive oil
1 tbsp fresh chopped tarragon
salt and pepper

Cook rice in boiling salted water for about 45 minutes, or until grains are tender. Drain and cool. Add other salad ingredients. Mix dressing ingredients. Stir through salad and serve.

Serves 2

CREATING A GOOD IMPRESSION

'Once you start exercising,' says *Bobby Davro*, 'you get hooked. A few years ago the ounces started to creep on. Since I'd just moved into a new house, I turned one bedroom into a gym and decided this was the year of the body.' The gym is a spacious, lushly-carpeted room with a bizarre iron contraption occupying about a quarter of it. This is the multi-gym. 'I automatically changed my diet, too,' he says with a groan. 'I gave up cake and all fried foods, including fish and chips. I have cereal for breakfast; lunch is usually a salad – I particularly like prawn salad; then I eat steak and salad, or fish or chicken for supper.'

HADDOCK IN MUSHROOM AND WATERCRESS SAUCE

Brainfood (fish) with a healthy low-fat mushroom sauce.

½ pint/300 ml skimmed milk
4 haddock fillets
1 oz/25 g low fat margarine
4 oz/100 g button mushrooms, wiped and sliced
½ oz/15 g flour
salt and pepper
1 tbsp watercress, chopped
1 lemon, sliced, 1 lime, sliced
watercress for garnish

Pour milk over fish in an ovenproof dish. Poach in oven at Gas 6/400°F/200°C for 10 minutes or until cooked. Remove haddock to serving dish and keep warm. Strain milk into jug.

Melt margarine in a saucepan and fry mushrooms for 2 minutes. Remove from heat and add flour. Gradually blend in milk. Return to heat and gently bring to boil, stirring until thickened. Season. Stir in watercress.

Pour sauce over fish and garnish with lemon-and-lime twists and fresh watercress.

Serves 4

FITNESS FISHY SALAD

Super luxury salad with prawns.

1 round lettuce, leaves separated
2 spring onions, in strips
½ red pepper, de-seeded and in strips
1 small courgette, in strips
12 oz/350 g peeled prawns
2 tbsp white wine vinegar
6 tbsp olive oil
½ tsp mustard
1 tbsp dill, chopped
salt and pepper
7 whole prawns to garnish

Line serving plate with lettuce. Top with vegetables and prawns. Blend vinegar, oil, mustard, dill, salt and pepper and pour over salad. Garnish with whole prawns.

Serves 4

Tomato Tone-ups

Big beef tomatoes filled with a tasty mixture of tuna, spring onions and mushrooms.

4 beef tomatoes, tops sliced off
4 oz/100 g button mushrooms, wiped and thinly sliced
7 oz/200 g tin tuna in brine, drained
4 spring onions, trimmed and finely chopped
2 oz/50 g green beans, trimmed, blanched and cut
    into 1 in/2.5 cm sticks
1 tbsp lemon juice
fresh ground black pepper

Scrape out pips and flesh from tomato. Fill with mushrooms, tuna, spring onions, green beans. Sprinkle over lemon juice and season with pepper.

Serves 4

Slinky Salad

Tender chicken strips in orange dressing.

3 oranges, peeled and cut into slices
2 chicken breasts, cooked, skinned and cut into thin
    strips
1 oz/25 g walnuts, halved
2 tbsp fresh squeezed orange juice
1 tbsp chives, finely chopped
fresh ground black pepper
few sprigs oregano to decorate

Arrange orange slices around serving plate. Place chicken strips in the centre in a fan. Scatter over walnuts.

Mix orange juice, chives and pepper. Pour over salad. Decorate with oregano sprigs.

Serves 4

Carrot and Almonds

Colourful salad of grated carrots and flaked almonds with a chive dressing.

3 large carrots, peeled and grated
4 oz/100 g flaked almonds
2 tbsp white wine vinegar
6 tbsp olive oil
1 tbsp chives, chopped
½ tsp Dijon mustard
salt and pepper

Mix carrots and almonds together and place on serving dish. Blend vinegar, oil, chives, mustard, salt and pepper and pour over.

Serves 4

CARA MIA KATE

To make a good impression on ace mimic *Kate Robbins*, all you need to do is present her with a fresh Italian salad and a plate of home-made pasta.
'I adore Italian food,' says Kate,' I love the whole Italian way of life. The way complete families from grannies to the kids all eat together. Every meal's a social occasion in that country.'
It was Kate's mum who introduced her to the delights of Italian cooking. 'When other kids were eating chips,' she says, 'my mother used to give us pasta. I love Spaghetti Bolognese.'
'To tell if spaghetti is ready, this is what you do,' reveals Kate. 'You fork out a strand and throw it at the wall. If it sticks, it's done!'

FLORENTINES

Delectable and delicate: crisp, fruity, cocktail biscuits.

2 oz/50 g unsalted butter
2 oz/50 g sugar
½ oz/15 g glacé cherries, chopped, and crystallised peel
1 oz/25 g crystallised pineapple, chopped
2 oz/50 g flaked almonds
1 tbsp double cream
6 oz/175 g plain chocolate

Melt butter, add sugar and bring to the boil. Remove from heat and add fruit and nuts. Stir in cream. Place teaspoons of mixture on a buttered baking sheet allowing room to spread. Bake at Gas 4/350°F/180°C until golden. Reassemble mixture into circles. Leave to cool on baking sheet. Remove.
   Melt chocolate in a bowl over a pan of simmering water. Spread chocolate on one side of biscuits and leave to set.

Makes 20

SPAGHETTI BOLOGNESE

Everyone's favourite pasta dish.

1 large onion, peeled and sliced
2 cloves garlic, crushed
2 tbsp oil
1 lb/450 g minced beef
2 tbsp tomato purée
15 oz/425 g tin tomatoes, chopped
1 bay leaf
1 tsp oregano
salt and pepper
8 oz/225 g spaghetti
1 tsp oil

For the Bolognese sauce, fry onion and garlic in oil until soft. Add mince and fry until browned. Stir in tomato purée and tomatoes. Season with bay leaf, oregano, salt and pepper. Cover and simmer for 30 minutes, stirring occasionally.
   Cook spaghetti in plenty of boiling salted water. Add oil to prevent sticking. Cook until just firm to the bite. Drain, and serve with Bolognese sauce.

Serves 4

RISOTTO CARA MIA

Easy rice dish with nuggets of chicken liver and green peppers.

8 oz/225 g chicken livers, tubes removed, chopped
1 green pepper, de-seeded and chopped
2 tbsp olive oil
1 onion, peeled and sliced
8 oz/225 g short grain rice
1 tsp turmeric
¾ pint/425 ml chicken stock
salt and pepper
1 bay leaf

Fry chicken livers and green pepper in oil for 5 minutes. Remove with slotted spoon. Add onion to pan and cook until soft but not browned. Stir in rice and turmeric followed by stock. Season with salt and pepper. Add bay leaf. Cook for 20-25 minutes or until rice is tender, adding extra water if necessary.

Serves 4

ZABAGLIONE

Traditional Italian whisked egg yolk dessert, flavoured with Marsala.

6 egg yolks
6 oz/175 g caster sugar
1 tsp finely grated lemon rind
1 tsp finely grated orange rind
½ pt/300 ml Marsala or sweet sherry
1 tsp lemon rind, finely grated to decorate

Whisk yolks with sugar and rind until pale in colour. Whisk in Marsala or sherry gradually. Place bowl over a pan of simmering water and whisk until mixture thickens. Pour into glasses and decorate with lemon rind.

Serves 4

TOMATO, MOZZARELLA AND AVOCADO SALAD

Fabulous appetiser of sliced cheese, tomato and avocado, dressed with fresh basil if you can get it.

4 small, firm tomatoes, cut into thin wedges
4 oz/100 g mozzarella cheese, cut into thin slices
2 ripe avocados, peeled, stoned and cut into thin slices
1 tsp lemon juice
4 sprigs basil leaves

Arrange tomatoes, mozzarella and avocados in a fan shape. Sprinkle a little lemon juice over avocado. Decorate with basil leaves.

Serves 4

Aspel's Italy

Saturday lunch in the Aspel household often means punching up some pasta dough on the kitchen table. Elder son, Patrick, sifts the flour into the bowl while the younger, Daniel, adds the eggs. Lizzie, *Michael Aspel*'s wife, trickles in the olive oil. Then the whole mixture is turned out and lots of hands start kneading and pounding, and everyone ends up with flour on their noses, paste-filled finger-nails and the backs of their jeans caked with raw dough. Good natured squabbles follow about who turns the handle of the pasta machine, which flattens the dough before it is wound through cutters to make tagliatelle or spaghetti. Family holidays by the lakes in Northern Italy have firmly established the Aspels' love of the country's food and wine. So here are a few of their suggestions to add an Italian flavour to mealtimes.

Florence Fennel

Chunky salad of fennel slices in tomato sauce with olives.

Tomato sauce
1 onion, peeled and chopped
1 clove garlic, crushed
3 tbsp olive oil
15 oz/425 g tin chopped tomatoes
salt and fresh ground black pepper
1 tsp sugar
1 tsp fresh basil, chopped

Salad
2 fennel bulbs, trimmed and sliced
1 tbsp lemon juice
2 oz/50 g black olives
sprig of fresh basil to garnish

Fry onion and garlic in oil until soft. Stir in tomatoes, salt, pepper, sugar and basil. Simmer for 10 minutes, then purée. Cool.
   Blanch fennel in a large pan of boiling water with lemon juice for 2 minutes. Drain and cool.
   Arrange fennel on a serving dish, spoon over sauce and decorate with olives and basil.

Serves 4

Home-made Pasta

Easy to make and you don't necessarily need a pasta machine. A sturdy rolling pin and a strong pair of wrists will do – so long as you roll out the pasta thinly.

8 oz/225 g strong plain flour
2 eggs, beaten
½ tsp salt
2 tbsp olive oil

Sift flour into a large bowl. Make a well in the centre, and add eggs, salt and oil. Mix to a soft dough, using hands. Knead lightly on a floured surface until smooth. Cover and rest in a cool place for 30 minutes. Halve and roll out to a large rectangle with a pasta machine or rolling pin. Cut to size. Leave to dry out over the back of a clean chair. Use for ravioli, lasagne, tagliatelle, etc.

Serves 4

FIGS AND APRICOTS IN RED WINE

Fresh fruits marinated in wine, for a refreshing Italian dessert.

¼ pint/150 ml water
¼ pint/150 ml red wine
4 oz/100 g granulated sugar
4 fresh figs, trimmed and sliced
6 apricots, halved and stoned

Pour water and wine into a large pan. Add the sugar and heat gently until sugar is completely dissolved. Bring the liquid to the boil and then reduce by half. Place the figs and the apricots in heatproof serving dish and then pour the hot wine syrup over the fruit. Cool before serving.

POLPETTINE

Herby meatballs in spinach sauce, served with fresh tagliatelle.

Meatballs
1 lb/450 g minced beef
1 small onion, peeled and finely chopped
1 clove garlic, crushed
½ tsp dried oregano
salt and fresh ground black pepper
1 small egg, beaten
flour for coating

Spinach sauce
4 oz/100 g defrosted chopped spinach
1 egg yolk
½ tsp freshly grated nutmeg
salt and freshly ground black pepper
¼ pint/150 ml plain yoghurt
10 oz/275 g fresh tagliatelle

Mix mince, onion, garlic, oregano, salt and pepper and enough egg to bind. Form into small balls and roll in flour to coat. Fry in a little oil until cooked through.

For sauce, drain excess liquid from spinach. Stir in yolk, nutmeg, salt and pepper. Pour into a pan and heat through gently.

Cook tagliatelle in a large pan of lightly salted boiling water until tender. Drain and serve with meatballs. Pour over sauce.

Serves 4

SPAGHETTI WITH PESTO SAUCE

Traditional, delicious green sauce made from basil, pine nuts, olive oil and Parmesan.

12 oz/350 g spaghetti
2 oz/50 g fresh basil leaves
2 oz/50 g fresh parsley
2 oz/50 g pine nuts
2 cloves garlic, peeled
6 fl oz/175 ml olive oil
2 oz/50 g fresh grated Parmesan cheese

Cook spaghetti in a large pan of boiling salted water for 12 minutes.

For the sauce, process the basil leaves, fresh parsley, pine nuts and garlic with half the oil. Stir in remaining oil and cheese.

Drain spaghetti and stir through pesto sauce.

Serves 4

OSSO BUCO

Country dish of slowly cooked shin of veal in white wine and tomato sauce.

1 onion, peeled and finely chopped
2 oz/50 g butter
2 lb/900 g shin of veal, cut into 2 in/5 cm slices
¼ pint/150 ml dry white wine
15 oz/425 g tin chopped tomatoes
¼ pint/150 ml beef stock
salt and fresh ground black pepper
chopped parsley to garnish

Fry onion in butter until soft. Add veal and fry until lightly browned. Stand veal upright in the pan so the marrow doesn't fall out of the bone. Add wine, tomatoes, stock and seasoning. Bring to boil, cover and simmer for 1½ hours or until veal is tender. Garnish with parsley.

Serves 4

Lizzie Aspel gives a helping hand with the home-made pasta.

Egg Dishes

The most useful and versatile product of nature which arrives intact in its own hygienic wrapping has to be the egg.
With half a dozen eggs in the larder you've always got the making of a meal. Whether it's an omelette, scrambled egg or poached egg on toast, you can be certain of a protein-packed pang reliever which is always fast to prepare.
So it's always a good idea to have a few eggstra ideas up your sleeve for a change. Here's a selection of star recipes to start you off.

EGG AND BACON BIFF

Crisp bacon and spaghetti stirred into beaten eggs. A knock-out super treat from *Frank Bruno*.

6 oz/150 g spaghetti
2 oz/50 g butter
1 medium onion, peeled and chopped
8 rashers bacon, de-rinded and chopped
6 eggs, beaten
salt and pepper

Cook spaghetti in boiling salted water for about 12 minutes or until just soft. Melt butter in a frying pan. Gently fry onion for a few minutes. Add bacon and fry until brown. Drain spaghetti. Stir in eggs, add bacon and onion and cook for 2 minutes until eggs scramble and cling to spaghetti strands. Season.

Serves 4

FINAL SCORE

An individual omelette cake stuffed with potatoes and peas from *Brian Moore*.

1 small onion, peeled and chopped
1 tbsp oil
1 small potato, cooked and diced
1 tbsp frozen peas
2 eggs, beaten
2 tsp water
salt and pepper

Fry onion in oil, in a 3 in/7.5 cm shallow pan until soft. Add potato, peas and heat through. Beat eggs with water and seasoning. Pour into pan and cook until set. Place under a hot grill to brown. Serve hot or cold.

Serves 1

ORGY OMELETTE

'This was a tasty thing I knocked up for Jackie Collins – quick and easy and just what the sex therapist ordered,' says *Max Headroom*.

2 oz/50 g mushrooms, wiped and sliced
1 oz/25 g butter
2 eggs, separated
2 tsp water
salt and pepper
1 tbsp oil
1 oz/25 g cream cheese
1 tomato, sliced for garnish

Fry mushrooms in butter for a few minutes. Mix egg yolks with water, salt and pepper in a bowl. Whisk egg whites until stiff and fold into egg yolks. Heat oil in a small frying pan. Spoon in egg mixture and smooth top. Fry for a few minutes until underside turns golden brown. Spread mushrooms and dot cream cheese over top. Fold over and heat through. Place on warmed serving plate and garnish with tomato.

Serves 1

SPANISH OMELETTE

Thick omelette cake served in wedges.

4 tbsp olive oil
1 large Spanish onion, peeled and sliced
4 large potatoes, cooked and sliced
salt and fresh ground black pepper
4 eggs, beaten
sliced tomato and sprig of parsley

Heat oil in a frying pan and fry onion until soft. Remove. Place half potatoes on bottom of pan in a layer. Add onions, then another layer of potatoes. Season layers. Pour over eggs. Cook slowly until eggs set. Turn out and cut into wedges. Garnish with tomato and parsley.

Serves 4

EGG FLIP

Eggy and alcoholic, this is a popular drink in Norway, brought to you by *Anneka Rice*.

8 egg yolks
1 egg white
2 tsp cold water
3 oz/75 g caster sugar
4 tbsp sweet sherry, or brandy

Beat egg yolks and white in a bowl. Add water and sugar and beat over a pan of simmering water, until pale and frothy. Pour 1 tbsp sherry or brandy into each tall stemmed glass, and top up with egg mixture. Serve immediately, with crisp, sweet biscuits.

Serves 4

At the end of a hard day's commentating, Brian Moore talks his way through to the Final Score – in this case an omelette cake.

SHEILAS

An unusual sandwich for the most romantic of occasions from actor *Jimmy Mulville*. Mash egg mayonnaise into a paste and spread on rye bread, then top with smoked oysters – available canned from delis and supermarkets – and garnish with lemon.

4 eggs, hardboiled and shelled
2 tbsp mayonnaise
salt and white pepper
4 small slices rye bread, lightly buttered
1 tin smoked oysters, drained
twist of lemon and mixed salad to serve

Finely chop eggs and mix with mayonnaise. Season with salt and pepper and spread over rye bread. Top with 3 oysters. Serve with lemon twist and salad.

Serves 4

Fist Food from Ruby Wax

Outrageous *Ruby Wax* can't understand why we Brits go on about food.
'All your pork pies and stodgy puds leave me cold,' she says.
'I love eating, but never cook,' says the girl who once opened the door of
her fan-assisted oven, was terrified by the typhoon that whooshed out,
and has never used it since. So if she's entertaining it will either be some
posh take-away food from a restaurant, which she'll be quite prepared to
pretend she made herself! Or more than likely, it'll be a batch of
burgers, hot dogs or fried chicken for guests to munch.

Curried Chicken Fists

Curried chicken in puff pastry pasties.

1 onion, peeled and chopped
1 clove garlic, crushed
1 oz/25 g butter
½ in/1cm piece ginger root, peeled and chopped
½ tsp turmeric
½ tsp chilli powder
½ tsp garam marsala
8 oz/225 g chicken, cubed
2 tomatoes, peeled and chopped
salt and pepper
13 oz/375 g packet frozen puff pastry, thawed
1 egg, beaten for glazing

Fry onion and garlic in butter until soft. Add ginger, turmeric, chilli, and garam marsala. Cook for 2 minutes. Add chicken and cool for 5 minutes, stirring. Add tomatoes and seasoning and gently fry until chicken is cooked. Cool.

   Roll out pastry thinly. Cover and rest for 30 minutes. Cut into 12 circles. Place a little mixture in the centre of 6 of the circles. Dampen the edges and seal with the remaining circles. Cut slits round edge and pierce top. Glaze. Bake on greased baking sheet at Gas 7/425°F/220°C for 15 minutes. Serve hot or cold.

Makes 6

Fishburgers

Chunky fishburgers and crisp salad topped with tartare sauce in sesame seed buns.

1 lb/450 g cod, cooked and flaked
8 oz/225 g potatoes, cooked and mashed
salt and pepper
2 eggs, beaten
4 oz/100 g white breadcrumbs
4 tbsp oil
6 sesame seed buns
6 crisp lettuce leaves washed
2 tomatoes, sliced
1 onion, cut into rings
2 tbsp tartare sauce

Mix together fish and potato. Season, and bind with half egg mix. Shape into 6 burgers on a lightly floured surface. Coat in remaining beaten egg, then breadcrumb. Heat oil in a large pan and fry both sides.

   Cut buns in half. Fill with lettuce, burger, tomato, onion and 1tsp each of tartare sauce.

Makes 6

DOUBLE-DECKER BURGERS

Two-tier beefburgers with salad garnish.

1½ lb/700 g minced beef
1 small onion, peeled and chopped
salt and pepper
½ tsp oregano
1 tbsp tomato purée
1 egg, beaten
4 white baps, each cut into three layers
2 gherkins, sliced
4 crisp lettuce leaves
4 tbsp mayonnaise

Place beef, onion, salt, pepper, oregano and tomato purée in a bowl. Bind ingredients together with the beaten egg. Divide mixture into 8 and mould into flat rounds. Grill both sides until cooked through. Place burgers between bap slices with gherkins, lettuce and mayonnaise. Serve with French fries.

Serves 4

All-American Double-Decker Burgers are Ruby Wax's standby.

SUGAR LIPS

Fast doughnuts for a sweet nothing.

8 oz/225 g plain flour
½ tsp bicarbonate of soda
1 tsp cream of tartar
1 oz/25 g butter
2 oz/50 g caster sugar
1 large egg, beaten
4 tbsp milk
2 oz/50 g granulated sugar for coating

Sift flour, bicarbonate of soda, cream of tartar into a bowl. Rub in butter and stir in sugar. Add beaten egg and milk and mix to a soft dough. Roll out on a floured surface until about ½ in/1 cm thick and cut out using a plain pastry cutter. Deep fry until golden brown, turning frequently. Remove and dip in sugar.

Makes 10

DALLAS FRIED CHICKEN

3 lb/1.4 kg chicken, cut into small portions, and
    skinned
2 eggs, beaten
8 oz/225 g fresh white breadcrumbs
salt and pepper

Dip chicken pieces in beaten egg. Season
breadcrumbs with salt and pepper, and coat
chicken. Deep fry until cooked through.

Serves 4

NIÇOISE BOAT

Filling and well-flavoured treat. A hunk of crusty
French bread stuffed with tasty goodies.

1 short French stick, halved lengthways
½ oz/15 g butter, softened
4 slices salami
4 black olives, stoned and halved
7 oz/200 g can tuna, drained and flaked
1 tsp capers
salt and freshly ground black pepper

Spread the inside of the French stick with butter.
Line with slices of salami and fill with olives,
flaked tuna and capers Season with salt and black
pepper and serve.

Serves 1

BLT

The legendary Californian bacon, lettuce and
tomato sandwich – a tasty snack for brunch or
supper.

1 oz/25 g butter, softened
3 slices wholemeal brown bread
2 rashers bacon, de-rinded and grilled crisp
2 crisp lettuce leaves
1 tomato, sliced
1 tbsp mayonnaise
salt and pepper

Spread butter over 3 slices of bread. Place bacon
on first layer of bread, then cover with second
slice. Top with lettuce, tomato, mayonnaise, salt
and pepper and remaining bread. Cut into
triangles and serve.

Serves 1

ITALIAN CONNECTION

Fried mozzarella and tomato sandwich. Hot, gooey
and scrumptious.

2 slices white bread
1 tomato, sliced
1 oz/25 g mozzarella cheese, sliced
2 basil leaves, chopped
salt and freshly ground black pepper
1tsp oil

Cut each slice of bread into a large round using a
cutter. Place tomato, mozzarella and basil on one
slice. Season with salt and pepper and cover with
other slice. Heat oil in a frying pan and fry
sandwich on both sides until golden brown.

Serves 1

HAT TRICK

Pitta bread stuffed with 3 delicious ingredients for
tasty, wholesome – and different – parcel.

7 oz/200 g tin red kidney beans, drained
7 oz/200 g tin cannellini beans, drained
7 oz/200 g tin tuna, drained and flaked
1 onion, finely chopped
1 tsp oregano
salt and pepper
6 crisp lettuce leaves, washed and dried
3 wholemeal pitta bread, halved

Mix beans and tuna together. Add onion, oregano,
and season. Fill pitta halves with lettuce and bean-
and-tuna.

Serves 6

GOLDEN CRUNCH

Fish steak in a bap for brainfood.

4 oz/100 g boneless white fish steak
1 egg, beaten
1 oz/25 g fresh brown breadcrumbs
salt and pepper
1 tbsp oil
1 bap, halved and toasted
1 tsp tartare sauce
½ small onion, cut into rings

Dip fish into egg, then breadcrumbs, and season.
Fry in oil until cooked through and golden. Place
in bap, and top with tartare sauce and onion rings.

Serves 1

ROLL CALL

Soft long roll with a spiced-up frankfurter wrapped
in ham. A real sausage special.

1 tsp made English mustard
1 slice ham
1 frankfurter sausage
1 long bridge roll, halved and lightly buttered
parsley

Spread mustard on ham and wrap around sausage.
Place in roll and garnish with parsley.

Serves 1

COOL CATS

Frankfurters in buns, decorated with spirals of
ketchup and mustard as seen above.

4 frankfurter sausages
4 long soft rolls
English mustard
tomato ketchup

Put frankfurters in a jug of hot water for 3 minutes
or until heated through. Cut rolls lengthways and
insert sausages. Top with mustard and tomato
sauce squirted from squeezy bottles.

Serves 4

CROQUE MONSIEUR

French fried sandwiches cut into triangles.

4 slices white bread, buttered
Dijon mustard
4 oz/100 g Cheddar cheese, grated
2 slices ham
oil and butter for frying

Spread buttered bread slices with mustard. Make 2
sandwiches with cheese and ham slices. Remove
crusts and cut into triangular halves. Fry quickly
in a mixture of oil and butter until they are brown
on both sides and the cheese starts to ooze out.

Serves 2

81

LONDON'S BEST

Traditional Cockney fare has always included jellied eels, cockles, fish
and chips, and pie and mash. And Kennington-born comic,
Gary Wilmot, is mad about them all.
'I've always loved fish and chips and pie and mash in particular,' he says.
'Coming home from school, I used to hop off the bus opposite a pie and
eel shop. I could never resist the temptation to nip inside and walk home
scoffing hot pie and mash with my fingers!'

DRESSED CRAB

Choose one small crab per person, or a monster
crab to share. Depending on the size of the
fishmonger's muscles, and the look on his face,
pick up the crab. If it feels heavy for its size, you
could be in luck. But shake it to make sure it's not
just full of water. Females have orange-coloured
coral, and males' innards are white and curdy.
Recognise them from their shells – the female has a
wide, fat tail folded underneath; the male's is
narrow and pointed.

To dress a crab, first twist off the big claws and
thin legs. Crack and remove all white meat with a
toothpick. Reserve it. Place crab on its back and
press down on the mouth with both thumbs until
you hear the fragile bones crack. Pull away and
discard mouth parts, and stomach attached
underneath. Next, pull out bony 'body' of the
crab. This is surrounded by grey, pointed inch-
long fronds – the crab's lungs or 'dead men's
fingers'. Pull off and discard. Crack 'body' in half.
Remove crab meat from nooks and crevices and
reserve with other white meat. Scoop out the
brown meat that lines the shell and mix with the
white meat. Now pile everything back into the
shell. Serve with brown bread and butter.

COCKLES

Tiny grey nuggets of sea-flavoured gristle with a
yellow point at one end. Douse in vinegar and eat
with a toothpick. Or buy the larger frozen variety
to use in seafood salads and fish pies.

MUSSELS

Orange- or buff-coloured fleshy bites in an elegant,
long bivalve, navy-blue shell. Buy them vinegar-
soaked from stalls. Or shake in a pan over a high
heat with chopped onion, parsley and wine or cider
and eat hot.

Always wash fresh mussels in cold water,
discarding any that remain open, or which do not
close when tapped with the back of a knife. After
cooking, discard any mussels which remain closed.

WHELKS

Whopping, thick, pointed shells from which you
uncoil these sea beasts. Sprinkle with vinegar.

PRAWNS AND SHRIMPS

Fresh-boiled plump pink prawns, or little brown
shrimps are sold by the pint. Peel away jointed
shell and eat with fingers.

WINKLES

A beautiful navy-blue, these tiny, round, glossy
shells belie the unsavoury-looking black worm
uncoiled by inserting a pin in the 'foot'. So long as
you keep your eyes closed, you could love them.
Gary Wilmot does.

Cockney comic Gary Wilmot tucking into Fish and Chips.

JELLIED EELS

Real old East End fare that you eat from a china bowl with a hunk of dry bread.

1 lb/450 g eel, in 1in/2 cm chunks
¾ pint/450 ml water
1 medium onion, peeled and thinly sliced
1 carrot, peeled and sliced
3 tbsp malt vinegar
salt
6 black peppercorns

Place eel in a pan and cover with water. Add rest of ingredients and bring to the boil. Cover and simmer for 15-20 minutes, removing any scum. Spooninto bowl. Strain stock and pour over. Cool, then chill. Stock will set like jelly. Serve cold.

Serves 4

FISH AND CHIPS

Use any white fish fillets, from rock salmon to plaice, about 8 oz/225 g per person.

2¼ lb/1 kg peeled potatoes
oil for deep frying
4 fish fillets

Batter
4 oz/100 g plain flour
1 tsp baking powder
½ tsp salt water

Sift flour into a bowl with baking powder and salt. Make a well in the middle and gradually beat in water until batter is the coating consistency of cream. Leave in the fridge for 30 minutes.

Cut potatoes into fat chips, about ½in/1 cm wide. Cover with cold water until needed, then drain and dry on kitchen paper.

Half-fill deep-fry pan with oil. Don't over-fill or it may bubble up and spill when you fry fish or chips. Heat oil. It's hot enough when a raw chip rises straight to the surface bubbling furiously.

Dip each fish fillet into batter, making sure it is well coated. Carefully lower into oil and cook until batter is crisp – about 8 minutes, depending on thickness of fish. Lower a frying basket half-full of chips into hot oil. Don't cook too many at once or temperature of oil will be reduced. Cook for about 5 minutes or until golden. Remove with basket or a draining spoon. Drain on kitchen paper and keep warm. Return to hot oil for 1-2 minutes just before serving.

Serves 4

PIE, MASH AND PARSLEY LIQUOR

Small pies made with traditional suet pastry and rich mince filling.

12 oz/350 g plain flour
6 oz/175 g grated suet
salt, water
2 tbsp oil
1 large onion, peeled and finely chopped
2 lb/900 g best lean mince
1 pint/600 ml beef stock (made with a stock cube)
salt and freshly ground black pepper
milk to glaze

Parsley liquor
1 pint/600 ml water
1 tbsp plain flour
6 tbsp fresh parsley, finely-chopped
1 tbsp grated onion
salt and white pepper

1½ lb/700 g cooked hot mashed potato

Sift flour, then stir in suet and salt. Gradually add water to make a dough. Knead lightly. Divide into 4. Reserving a third of each piece for a lid, roll out to ¼ in/0.5 cm and line 4 greased individual pie tins, or dishes.

Heat oil in pan and fry onion soft, but not brown. Add mince and fry until brown. Stir in stock, add salt and pepper. Bring to the boil, then simmer until gravy thickens. Cool.

Fill pastry-lined dishes with mince. Roll out and cut a pastry lid to fit. Dampen edges and press on top of pie dish. Brush with milk to glaze. Bake at Gas 6/400°F/200°C for about 15 minutes until cooked.

To make the parsley liquor, stir water into flour. Add parsley and onion. Bring to the boil stirring, until liquor thickens. Season.

Serve hot pie with two scoops of mash, a ladle of liquor with a dash of vinegar.

Serves 4

Desserts

For the sweet-toothed, these puddings from your favourite TV stars add the perfect finishing touch to a meal. Choose a light airy mousse or a fruit trifle for a summer dessert, or to help warm you up on a cold winter's day choose from traditional puds like Treacle Tarts, a Jam Roly Poly or Rice Pudding.

Fresh Fruit Kebabs – the perfect complement to a summer's day from Angela Thorne.

Angela Thorne grew up in the foothills of the Himalayas, the land of the pomelo and mango. So it's not surprising she has retained a love of fresh fruit. Here are three of her favourites.

FRESH FRUIT KEBABS

Colourful fresh fruit chunks on sticks.

4 fresh apricots, halved and stones removed
2 kiwi fruit, cut into chunks
8 strawberries, wiped
4 dates, halved and stones removed
1 Sharon fruit, sliced

Thread fruit onto wooden skewers. Chill before serving.

Serves 4

ST CLEMENT'S SALAD

Vitamin C-packed salad of mixed citrus fruits.

1 pink grapefruit
1 grapefruit
6 navel oranges, peeled and sliced
1 pomelo, peeled and sliced
4 oz/100 g kumquats, thinly sliced

Remove peel and pith from grapefruits. Cut into segments removing pips and reserving any juices. Mix fruit together with juices. Pile into a glass serving bowl and chill before serving.

Serves 6

MELON BASKET

Hollowed water melon filled with mixed melon and cucumber balls.

1 small water melon
1 galia melon
1 canteloupe melon
½ cucumber, peeled and cut into balls
2 tbsp sherry
1 tbsp soft brown sugar
mint leaves to garnish

Shape water melon into a basket by cutting out portions, leaving a handle. Cut remaining melons in half, discard pips, then scoop flesh into balls. Mix melon and cucumber together, pour over sherry and sprinkle with sugar. Garnish with mint leaves.

Serves 4

APRICOT MOUSSE

'I've ordered this for Vidal Sassoon. He didn't know whether to eat it or rub it in his hair. Either way it's delicious,' says *Max Headroom.*

2 oz/50 g caster sugar
2 eggs, separated
1 sachet gelatine, soaked in 3 tbsp water
1 lb/450 g tin of apricots, drained
½ pint/300 ml double cream

Beat sugar and egg yolks until light and thick. Dissolve gelatine in a bowl over hot water. Allow to cool slightly. Purée apricots and beat into sugar and egg mixture. Stir in gelatine. Whip cream until thick and fold into apricot mixture, followed by stiffly beaten egg whites.

Pour mixture into a greased 2 pint/1.2 litre mould and chill until set. Immerse in hot water for a few seconds, and turn out onto a serving dish. Decorate with fresh flowers.

Serves 6

CRÈME CLAPHAM

This creamy, light pud made simply from blackcurrants puréed with crème fraîche and double cream is a favourite of *Jimmy Mulville.*

8 oz/225 g blackcurrants
¼ pint/150 ml crème fraîche
¼ pint/150 ml double cream, lightly whipped
sugar to taste
mint leaves and wafer biscuits to serve

Purée blackcurrants. Fold into crème fraiche and cream. Add sugar to taste. Spoon into 4 small ramekin dishes, smooth top and chill. Decorate with mint leaves and serve with biscuits.

Serves 4

CUSTARDICUS HONICUS

Ancient, but delectable recipe for a creamy custard dessert much scoffed by actor *Rory McGrath.*

1 pint/600 ml milk
2 tbsp honey
4 eggs, beaten
½ tsp nutmeg

Gently heat milk and honey until honey has melted. Put eggs in a bowl and gradually whisk in milk and honey. Strain into an ovenproof dish, sprinkle with nutmeg and bake at Gas 2/300°F/150°C for 1 hour or until set.

Serves 4

ORANGE SYLLABUB

A pud expert, actor *Jonathan Newth* likes this quick, easy and fabulously orangey dessert.

1 orange
4 fl oz/100 ml medium dry white wine
3 tbsp caster sugar
½ pint/300 ml double cream

Thinly pare ribbons of orange peel, then cut into thin 'julienne' strips. Blanch in boiling water for 1½ minutes. Drain. Squeeze juice from orange and place in a bowl. Add wine and caster sugar and gradually whisk in cream until softly thick. Spoon into small glasses, decorate with orange julienne strips and chill.

Serves 6

DEAD DOG'S EYES

Roy Kinnear, grown-up but with a schoolboy's passions, enjoys these delicious trifles. Miss out sherry for the under-aged.

4 oz/100 g trifle sponges, or left-over sponge cake
15 oz/425 g can gooseberries, drained
6 tbsp sherry
¼ pint/150 ml milk
1 tsp cornflour
1 oz/25 g sugar
2 eggs yolks, beaten
1 drop vanilla essence
½ pint/300 ml whipping cream
1 glacé cherry.

Fit sponge cake into base of 6 ramekins. Spoon a few gooseberries into each, then sprinkle sherry over. Leave to soak.

Mix milk, cornflour and sugar in a bowl, over a pan of simmering water. Bring mixture to the boil and pour a little into well-beaten egg yolks. Mix well, return egg mixture to milk and cook until thick. Stir in vanilla essence. Cool.

Spoon custard over gooseberries. Whip cream until thick. Pipe rosettes over top. Decorate with chopped cherry.

Makes 6

SUNBEAMS

Fresh fruit salad served in orange shells which *Benny Hill* says is delicious. Looks very pretty, too!

2 oranges
2 oz/50 g green seedless grapes, halved
1 kiwi fruit, peeled and cut into chunks
2 clementines, peeled and broken into segments
1 red apple, cored and cut into chunks

Halve oranges and scoop out flesh, saving as much juice as possible. Add the fruits to the juice and then spoon into orange shells.

Serves 4

Orange Syllabub.

GARLAND GREEN TRIFLE

This pretty trifle from *Larry Grayson* has green fruits showing through the sides of the glass bowl.

6 trifle sponges, or left-over sponge cake
12 oz/350 g can gooseberries
4 tbsp sherry
4 oz/100 g green grapes, halved and pips removed
2 kiwi fruit, peeled and sliced
½ green apply, cored and sliced
14 oz/400 g can custard
few drops green colouring
½ pint/300 ml double cream
1 kiwi fruit, peeled and sliced, to decorate

Place trifle sponges in the bottom of a large glass bowl. Pour over gooseberries and juice and add sherry. Leave to soak for 10 minutes. Add grapes, kiwi fruit and apple. Tint custard with green colouring and pour over fruit. Whisk cream until thickened, and pour over custard. Decorate with halved slices of kiwi fruit around edges.

Serves 6

Two scrumptious puddings greatly enjoyed by *Keith Barron*

RED FRUIT SALAD

It could also be green or yellow fruit salad – simply use as many different fruits of the same colour as you can find and layer in a glass dish so you can see it through the sides.

8 oz/225 g strawberries, hulled and sliced
2 red apples, cored and sliced
1 lb/450 g fresh or frozen raspberries
1 lb/450 g red plums, stoned and sliced

Place a layer of strawberries in the bottom of a glass dish. Top with a layer of red apple, skin outwards, then a layer of raspberries, a layer of plums, and so on to the top of the dish. Serve on its own with a liberal sprinkling of Grand Marnier. Or leave for 2 hours and serve in its own juice.

Serves 4

ORANGE BRANDY SYLLABUB

This lovely boozy pud used to be a more liquid dish much enjoyed by Charles II. He favoured the method of milking a cow directly into a bowl of warmed and sweetened wine!

rind and juice of 1 small orange
2 oz/50 g caster sugar
2 tbsp brandy
2 tbsp sherry
½ pint/300 ml double cream
orange peel curls for decoration

Put rind and orange juice into a bowl with sugar, brandy and sherry and leave to marinate. Strain liquid into a clean bowl. Add cream and beat well until mixture stands in peaks. Pour into glasses and chill overnight. Decorate with orange peel curls.

Serves 4

WIBBLY WOBBLY

Roy Kinnear's nostalgic schoolboy memories include a plate of this special fresh fruit juice jelly packed with fruit.

1 pint/600 ml water
3 oz/75 g caster sugar
1½ oz/40 g gelatine
6 oranges, washed and dried
1 lemon, washed and dried
1 banana, peeled and sliced
2 blood oranges, peeled and segmented
2 clementines, peeled and segmented
1 kiwi fruit, peeled, sliced, cut into four
2 oz/50 g green grapes, halved, with pips removed
1 red apple, cored and chopped

Put water and sugar in a pan and sprinkle over gelatine. Leave to soak. Cut thin strips of rind from 3 oranges, avoiding white pith. Add strips to pan and heat gently, without boiling. Cover and leave to infuse for 10 minutes. Squeeze juice from oranges and lemon and pour into mixture. Strain jelly into a large jug, discarding peel. Lightly oil a 2 pint/1.2 litre jelly mould. Mix fruit and place one third in the bottom of mould. Pour over one third of jelly. Allow to set in fridge. Repeat with remaining two thirds. When set, dip in hot water for a few seconds and turn out on to serving plate.

Makes 1½ pints/850 ml

Denis Norden's answer to wrecked meringues – Concorde Crunch.

Self-confessed clot in the kitchen, *Denis Norden* ruined a cake and wrecked the meringues, but all was not lost. SECOND-CHANCE TRIFLE and CONCORDE CRUNCH were the results.

SECOND-CHANCE TRIFLE

Traditional trifle made extra good using a thumbs-down cake as the base. Top with pomegranate seeds for a pretty decoration.

1 ruined sponge cake, burned parts trimmed
5 tbsp sherry
2×5 oz/150 g tins apricots halvesin syrup
1 blancmange mix, made according toinstructions
½ pint/300 ml whipping cream, lightly whipped
seeds from a pomegranate

Trim sponge to fit base of trifle dish. Pour over sherry. Drain syrup from apricots and pour ¼ pint/150 ml over sponge. Soak for 30 minutes. Purée drained apricots. Pour over sponge. Pour blancmange over next. Leave to cool. Top with cream. Sprinkle pomegranate seeds over the top.

Serves 8

CONCORDE CRUNCH

A supersonic pud from broken meringues. Use any selection of dried or glacé fruit. Below is simply a suggestion.

1 batch spoilt meringues
1 pint/600 ml double cream
2 oz/50 g sultanas
2 oz/50 g dried apricots, chopped
1 oz/25 g dried figs, chopped
1 oz/25 g glacé cherries, chopped
2 oz/50 g flaked almonds
2 oz/50 g soft brown sugar
4 oz/100 g raspberries, puréed

Crush meringues. Whip cream until thick. Fold in meringues, sultanas, apricots, figs, cherries and brown sugar. Add 1 oz/25 g almonds. Spoon into serving glasses and pour over raspberry purée. Decorate with remaining almonds.

Serves 4

GIDDY ORANGES

Sliced oranges with a caramel syrup from *Larry Grayson*. Try his recipe for BOULES too.

8 small oranges
1 lb/450 g sugar
½ pint/300 ml water
6 cloves
2 tbsp water
2 tbsp Cointreau

Thinly peel rind from 2 oranges, and cut into thin strips. Plunge strips into boiling water for 2 minutes. Drain and put to one side. Remove peel and pith from oranges and leave fruit whole. Pour any juice into a cup. Dissolve sugar in water over a low heat. Add cloves, bring to boil and simmer until it turns brown. Remove from heat and carefully add water, orange juice and Cointreau. Pour over oranges in a heatproof serving bowl and chill. Decorate with strips of peel.

Serves 4

BOULES

A refreshing fruit salad of melon, cucumber and strawberries, sprinkled with mint, served in the melon skins.

2 honeydew melons, halved and de-pipped
1 cucumber, peeled and cut with a melon baller
8 oz/225 g strawberries, hulled
2 tbsp mint, finely chopped

Scoop out melon flesh with a melon baller. Scrape out remaining flesh with a spoon leaving a ¼ in/ 0.5 cm border. Fill with melon and cucumber balls and strawberries. Sprinkle the chopped mint over and serve.

Serves 4

SWEETHEARTS

An outrageous pud from *Larry Grayson* who never cooks himself, but enjoys all the treats concocted by sister Fan. These jellies are made with claret and are strictly for grown-ups.

4 oz/100 g granulated sugar
¼ pint/150 ml water
8 oz/225 g redcurrant jelly
grated rind and juice of 1 lemon
grated rind and juice of 1 orange
½ pint/300 ml claret
1 sachet of gelatine, soaked in 2 tbsp water
mint leaves to decorate

Put sugar and water in a pan. Add redcurrant jelly, rind and juice from lemon and orange. Heat gently, stirring until sugar and jelly has melted. Strain into a clean pan. Add claret. Melt gelatine in a bowl over a pan of hot water. Stir into claret mixture. Oil 4 heart-shaped moulds and pour jelly into each. Leave in fridge to set.

Dip base of moulds quickly into hot water before turning out jellies. Decorate with mint leaves.

Serves 4

KANGEROOLADE

'Named as a tribute to our most famous marsupial,' says *Dame Edna*.

5 eggs
6 oz/175 g caster sugar
6 oz/175 g dark chocolate
½ pint/300 ml double cream, whipped
sifted icing sugar

Separate eggs. Beat yolks and sugar with an electric whisk until thick and creamy. Melt chocolate in a bowl over a pan of simmering water. Stir into egg yolks. Whisk whites until stiff, and carefully fold into mixture.

Line a Swiss-roll tin with buttered greaseproof paper; pour in mixture and spread evenly. Bake at Gas 5/375°F/190°C for 20 minutes or until just firm to touch. Cool for 10 minutes.

Turn out the sponge on to greaseproof paper, sprinkled with icing sugar. Spread over cream, leaving 1 in/2.5 cm gap down the long edge. Roll up carefully from short edge. Sprinkle with icing sugar.

Serves 6

Larry Grayson's weakness is his sweet tooth.

SWEET TALK

Just a schoolboy at heart who scoffs puds and stuffs stodge, wiry *Lionel Blair* says, 'I never put on an ounce!' At 6 ft tall, his weight is a constant 10½ stones, and he claims he can wear clothes he bought 20 years ago – he still has a 28 in waist. Which is so unfair when you look at his diet. He adores food – loves and savours every mouthful – and leans back rolling his eyes in ecstasy at the recollection of a particular favourite. His real indulgence is puds. 'As soon as I go into a restaurant,' he says, 'my eyes go straight to the dessert trolley. I can't resist puddings, the stodgier the better. There is absolutely nothing to beat bread and butter pudding, treacle tart, creamy rice, jam roly poly, suet pud . . . '

JAM ROLY POLY

Lovely jammy pastry roll, crisp on the outside and gooey in the middle

8 oz/225 g plain flour
pinch salt
2 oz/50 g margarine
2 oz/50 g lard
6 tbsp cold water
4 round tbsp strawberry jam
1 egg, beaten
1 tbsp caster sugar

Sift flour and salt into large bowl. Rub in fats and bind with water. Mix to a soft dough and wrap in cling film. Place in fridge for 30 minutes.

Roll out pastry to a large rectangle. Warm jam and spread evenly over pastry. Roll like a Swiss roll, place on a greased baking sheet, brush with beaten egg and sprinkle with sugar. Leave to rest for 30 minutes and then cook at Gas 6/400°F/200°C for about 30 minutes.

Serves 4

TREACLE TART

Sticky, syrupy filling in a crumbly pastry case.

6 oz/175 g plain flour, sifted
pinch salt
3 oz/75 g butter
2-3 tbsp iced water
6 fl oz/175 ml golden syrup
1 tbsp black treacle
juice and grated rind of ½ lemon
pinch nutmeg
8 oz/225 g fresh breadcrumbs
2 tbsp soured cream

Put flour and salt in a bowl and rub in fat until mixture resembles breadcrumbs. Stir in water to make a dough. Wrap and rest for 30 minutes, then use it to line an 8 in/20 cm flan dish.

In a small saucepan, warm syrup, treacle, lemon juice and rind, and stir in nutmeg. Remove from heat, cool, then stir in crumbs and soured cream. Pour into pastry case and then bake the tart at Gas 7/425°F/220°C for 20 minutes until pastry is golden brown.

Serves 4

BREAD AND BUTTER PUDDING

Wholesome variation of the Old English pud using wholemeal bread, brown sugar and spices.

12 thin slices brown bread, buttered, and crusts removed
1 pint/600 ml milk
2 eggs, beaten
1 oz/25 g brown sugar
2 oz/50 g sultanas
grated rind of 1 lemon and 1 orange
½ tsp cinnamon

Cut each bread slice into 4 squares. Arrange in layers in a buttered pie dish. Sprinkle each layer with sugar, sultanas, rind, fruit and spices. Pour over eggs and milk. Leave to stand for 1 hour to soak. Bake at Gas 4/350°F/180°C for 1 hour or until crisp on the top. Serve with custard.

Serves 4

PEKING TOM

Scrummy rice pudding, enriched with cream and eggs, served with puréed raspberries.

3 oz/75 g pudding rice
½ pint/300 ml milk
2 oz/50 g caster sugar
grated rind of 1 lemon
1 egg, beaten
½ pint/300 ml single cream
½ tsp nutmeg
8 oz/225 g frozen raspberries, defrosted and puréed.

Wash rice. Place in saucepan with milk, sugar and lemon rind. Bring to boil and simmer gently for 10 minutes. Put in ovenproof dish. Stir in egg and cream. Sprinkle over nutmeg. Bake at Gas 3/325°F/160°C for 1 hour. Serve with puréed raspberries.

Serves 6

JUNKET

Old-fashioned nursery dessert made with milk set with rennet.

1 pint/600 ml milk
1 rennet tablet or junket powder
1 tsp caster sugar
½ lime, thinly sliced

Warm milk to blood heat (feels neither hot nor cold to clean finger). Pour into serving dish and add sugar. Stir in rennet or junket powder. Leave in warm place to set (about 1½ hours). Decorate with lime slices.

Serves 4

PURE BRIBERY

Old-style apple pie.

8 oz/225 g plain flour
pinch salt
2 oz/50 g butter
2 oz/50 g lard
3-4 tbsp cold water
2 lb/900 g Bramley cooking apples, peeled, cored and diced
squirt of lemon juice
few whole cloves
4 tbsp caster sugar
1 egg, beaten
custard to serve

Sieve flour and salt into a bowl. Rub in fat to breadcrumb stage. Make a well in the centre and add enough water to make a soft dough. Knead lightly, wrap and chill for 30 minutes.

Divide pastry into 2 pieces. Roll out thinly on a lightly floured board. Cover a lightly buttered pie plate with one half and trim the edges. Spread apple on top, sprinkle with lemon juice, cloves and 3 tbsp sugar. Dampen edges, cover with remaining pastry, trim and seal.

Cut out letters to spell 'Apple Pie' with pastry trimmings, dampen and secure on top of the pie. Brush with egg and sprinkle over remaining sugar. Bake at Gas 6/400°F/200°C for 25-30 minutes or until pastry is golden. Serve with custard.

Serves 6

Lionel Blair thinks Jam Roly Poly gets top marks.

APRICOT SUET PUD

Fluffy rib-sticker with oozy jam creeping down the sides, made quickly in the microwave.

4 oz/100 g self-raising flour
2 oz/50 g suet
2 oz/50 g caster sugar
1 egg
4 tbsp milk approx (to give a sloppy dough)
4 tbsp apricot jam

Put flour, suet, sugar and egg into a large bowl and mix until blended. Pour in milk and beat to give a sloppy mixture. Spoon jam into the base of a greased 1 pint/600 ml plastic bowl, cover with dough mix, and microwave on high for 4 minutes. Stand for 1 minute, then turn out on to a warmed dish.

Serves 4

TOM FOOLERY

Gyles Brandreth is TV-am's favourite fool, but according to Gyles, being a fool is a pretty serious business – especially first thing in the morning. A great deal of stumbling about often results in some unintentional foolery, like treading barefoot into cat Oscar's breakfast. But being the caring and rather loveable fool he is, Gyles first job on waking is to make a cup of de-caffeinated tea for his long-suffering wife, Michele. 'Michele,' says Gyles, 'is as beautiful as Helen of Troy, has the brilliance of Jane Austen, the intelligence of Albert Einstein, and the culinary skills of Escoffier.' Fools of the edible kind, like these, are often on Michele's menus.

FOOLPROOF

Easy and irresistible pale green sensuous pud.

1 lb/450 g gooseberries
4 tbsp caster sugar
1 pint/600 ml double cream, lightly whipped

Wash and dry gooseberries and reserve a few for decoration. Purée remainder with sugar until smooth. Spoon a little purée into the bottom of each glass. Fold cream into remaining purée, and spoon into glasses. Slice remaining gooseberries to decorate tops.

Serves 4

FOOL'S PARADISE

4 nectarines, stoned and chopped
juice of ½ orange
1 tbsp sherry
12 oz/350 g crème fraîche
orange segments and nectarine slices, to decorate

Poach nectarines in orange juice and sherry until they are softened. Purée, then leave to cool. Spoon a little purée into the bottom of each glass. Fold crème fraîche into remaining purée. Spoon into tall glasses and decorate with orange and nectarine segments for a stylish and succulent finish.

SPOOF

This is a super stripy fool – so simple the kids can make it.

8 oz/225 g raspberries
2 tsp caster sugar
1 pint/½ litre tub raspberry ripple ice cream
raspberry syrup

Reserve a few raspberries for decoration. Purée remainder with sugar. Arrange scoops of ripple ice cream in serving bowl, layered with raspberry purée. Drizzle over syrup, and decorate with whole raspberries.

Serves 4

CUSTARD CLOWN

Traditional plum fool made with custard – buy a tinned custard from the supermarket if you don't have the time to make your own.

½ pint/300 ml milk
1 tsp cornflour
2 tbsp sugar
4 egg yolks, beaten
few drops vanilla essence
1 lb/450 g red plums, stoned and washed

Jest a fool or two from Gyles Brandreth!

Mix a little milk with cornflour to make a paste. Add remaining milk and sugar. Pour into a pan and gradually bring to the boil, stirring all the time. Pour a little of the milk over the egg yolks and stir. Pour back into the pan and gently heat, stirring until thickened. Do not allow to boil. Add vanilla essence. Cover with dampened greaseproof paper and leave to cool. Put plums in a blender, reserving a couple for decoration, and whizz until smooth. Fold into custard and spoon into glasses. Decorate with reserved plums.

Serves 4

BLUEBERRY BUFFOON

Deep purple fool that's frozen like ice cream. Serve in scoops and decorate with whole blueberries.

1 lb/450 g tin blueberries
2 oz/50 g caster sugar
1 pint/600 ml double cream, lightly whipped

Reserve a few of the blueberries for decoration and purée the remainder with the juice and sugar. Fold in cream and pour into a rigid freezer container. Cover and freeze until firm. Make sure the mixture is removed from the freezer 30 minutes before required. Scoop into serving glasses using an ice cream scoop. Decorate with reserved blueberries.

Serves 4

JESTER

Thick and creamy fool with Greek yoghurt, honey and dates.

1 lb/450 g tub Greek yoghurt
2 tbsp runny honey
8 oz/225 g dates, stoned and chopped
1 oz/25 g flaked almonds, toasted

Mix yoghurt, honey and dates, spoon into small glasses and sprinkle over almonds to serve.

Serves 4

Cakes

The delicious aroma of a cake baking is one of the most tantalising temptations to resist. Whilst it is easy these days to go out and buy a cake, why not take a tip from the stars: go to a little trouble and make one of these delectable recipes. An 'all-star' cake will help to make any occasion extra special.

Mollie Sugden first found fame as a baker when she cooked birthday cakes for her twin sons. Later her reputation spread and she was always the one to make cakes and treats for her fellow actors. Here are two particular favourites.

LUXURY CHEESECAKE

4 oz/100 g butter
8 oz/225 g digestive biscuits, crushed
4 eggs, separated
4 oz/100 g caster sugar
8 oz/225 g cottage cheese
8 oz/225 g soft cream cheese
1 tsp vanilla essence

Topping
½ pint/300 ml soured cream
2 tbsp caster sugar
½ tsp vanilla essence

Melt butter and stir in crushed biscuits. Press into the base and up the sides of a greased 8 in/ 20 cm round loose-bottomed tin.

Whisk egg yolks and sugar until thick. Sieve cottage cheese and stir into mixture with cream cheese and vanilla essence. Whisk egg whites and fold in. Pour mixture into biscuit base. Bake at Gas 4/350°F/180°C for 35-40 minutes.

For topping, mix together soured cream, sugar and vanilla and pour over the top.

Bake at Gas 8/450°F/230°C for 7 minutes. Cool in tin before removing.

Serves 8

MOLLIE'S COFFEE GATEAU

8 oz/225 g butter
8 oz/225 g caster sugar
4 eggs
10 oz/275 g self-raising flour, sifted
3 tbsp strong black coffee

Butter icing
4 oz/100 g butter
8 oz/225 g icing sugar, sifted
1 tbsp coffee essence

Glacé icing
2 tbsp warm water, approx
1 tsp coffee essence
6 oz/150 g icing sugar, sifted

½ pint/300 ml double cream, whipped
walnut halves

Cream the butter and sugar together. Beat in the eggs. Fold in the flour and the coffee. Spoon into greased, lined 8 in/20 cm cake tin. Bake at Gas 5/ 375°F/190°C for 40-45 minutes. Cool, remove from tin and complete cooling. Cut across in 3 layers. Beat butter soft, add icing sugar and coffee essence. Spread over 2 layers of cake and sandwich together.

For glacé icing, stir water and coffee essence into icing sugar. Pour over cake. Decorate with cream and walnuts.

Serves 8

Larry Grayson does not deny for one moment his sweet tooth. Try these scrumptious puds from his collection.

Sunday tea with Mollie Sugden and her husband William Moore.

EVERARD'S BUN

Choux bun ring, topped with flaked almonds and filled with coffee-flavoured cream.

2 oz/50 g butter
¼ pint/150 ml water
2½ oz/65 g plain flour, sifted
2 eggs, beaten
2 oz/50 g flaked almonds
½ pint/300 ml double cream
1 tsp strong liquid coffee
1 oz/25 g icing sugar, sifted

Melt butter in water in a pan. Bring to boil, remove from heat and tip flour into pan all at once. Beat with wooden spoon until paste is smooth and forms a ball. Cool, gradually mixing eggs into paste, beating well to give a glossy mixture of piping consistency. Cool. Fill a piping bag fitted with a large plain nozzle. Pipe a large ring on a greased baking sheet. Sprinkle nuts over ring. Bake at Gas 6/400°F/200°C for 10 minutes, then turn down to Gas 5/375°F/190°C for a further 10-15 minutes, or until golden. Cool on wire rack. Beat cream, coffee and icing sugar until thick. Split ring in half, fill with coffee cream. Replace top.

Serves 6

LARRY'S CHOCOLATE REFRIGERATOR CAKE

Irresistible cake studded with cherries and raisins – no cooking needed!

8 oz/225 g butter
6 oz/175 g golden syrup
8 oz/225 g plain chocolate
4 oz/100 g glacé cherries, chopped
4 oz/100 g raisins
12 oz/350 g digestive biscuits, crushed
4 oz/100 g plain chocolate
4 glacé cherries, halved

Grease an 8 in/20 cm loose-bottomed cake tin. Put butter, syrup, 8 oz/225 g chocolate into a bowl over a pan of hot water. Heat until butter and chocolate has melted. Remove from heat and stir in cherries, raisins and biscuits. Press mixture into tin and leave in a cool place to set. Melt remaining chocolate in a pan over hot water, pour over cake and leave to set again. Chill. Remove from tin and decorate with cherries. Serve in slices.

Serves 6

WALNUT BREAD

Keith Barron's wife Mary's super recipe for this delicious nutty bread. Eat with unsalted butter – or just as it is.

3 lb/1.4 kg wholemeal flour
1½ tsp salt
1 oz/25 g dried yeast
1½ tsp honey dissolved in 1¾ pint/1 litre lukewarm water
7 oz/200 g chopped walnuts

Mix flour, salt and yeast in a warmed bowl. Stir in water and honey mix to make a soft dough. Gather together and turn on to worktop. Knead for 5 minutes until smooth and elastic. Knead in walnuts, making sure they are evenly distributed. Halve the mixture. Put in 2 greased 2 lb/1 kg loaf tins. Cover and leave in a warm place until dough rises to the top of the tin. Bake in a pre-heated oven Gas 8/450°F/230°C for 5 minutes. Reduce heat to Gas 6/400°F/200°C and bake for 30 minutes more, or until loaves are cooked and sound hollow when tapped on the bottom.

Makes 2 loaves

TIPOVER CAKE

This is *Max Headroom's* own variation on Tipsy Cake, specially planned for when he entertained Oliver Reed.

5 oz/150 g caster sugar
5 oz/150 g butter
3 eggs
8 oz/225 g plain flour
pinch of salt
level tsp baking powder
6 tbsp brandy
15 oz/425 g tin of pineapple rings, drained
6 glacé cherries, washed and dried

Cream sugar and butter until light and fluffy. Beat in eggs, one at a time. Sieve flour, salt and baking powder together and fold into mixture, with 2 tbsp brandy and one chopped pineapple ring. Spoon into a greased and line 7 in/18 cm round cake tin. Smooth surface. Arrange halved pineapple rings around the edge, and one whole ring in the middle. Decorate with whole cherries. Cook at Gas 5/375°F/190°C for 1 hour 15 minutes. Leave in tin for 10 minutes before turning out on a wire rack to cool. Spoon over remaining brandy.

Serves 8

Actress *Siobhan Redmond* pictured opposite has an enviable figure, which belies her craving for cakes, scones and shortbread from Aunties Nessie and Cathie.

SHORTBREAD CRUICKSHANK

Buttery, melt-in-the-mouth crumbly biscuit.

8 oz/200 g butter
4 oz/100 g caster sugar
3 oz/75 g cornflour
9 oz/250 g plain flour
extra caster sugar for dredging

Cream butter and sugar. Stir in cornflour and flour a spoonful at a time. Mould into a ball, then press into a lightly-greased shortbread plate. Bake in pre-heated oven, Gas 4/350°F/180°C, for 45 minutes. Cool, turn out, then mark into sections. Dredge with sugar.

Serves 4

DUNDEE CAKE

Irresistible tea-time cake full of fruit and nuts.

8 oz/225 g soft margarine
8 oz/225 g caster sugar
grated rind of 1 orange
5 eggs
11 oz/300 g plain flour, sifted
1 tsp mixed spice
2 oz/50 g chopped almonds
1½ lb/700 g dried mixed fruit
2 oz/50 g glacé cherries, quartered, washed and dried
4 oz/100 g mixed cut peel
2 oz/50 g whole blanched almonds, for decoration

Grease and line 8 in/20 cm round cake tin. Pre-heat oven to Gas 2/300°F/150°C.

Cream margarine and sugar in a bowl until light and fluffy. Add orange rind. Beat in eggs one at a time, adding a little flour with each egg. Fold in remaining flour, spice, fruit and nuts until well mixed. Spoon mixture into tin, smooth top and decorate with almonds. Stand tin on top of several sheets of newspaper, and tie newspaper round the sides to prevent excessive browning and drying.

Bake the cake for 3½-4 hours or until an inserted skewer comes out clean. If cake browns too quickly, place greaseproof paper over the top halfway through cooking. Remove from oven and leave in tin for 10 minutes before turning out.

Makes 12 slices

CATHIE'S WEE SCONES

Tiny, light-as-a-feather scones, delicious with butter and jam.

2½ oz/60 g butter
8 oz/225 g self-raising flour
1 level tsp cream of tartar
½ tsp baking powder
1 tbsp sugar
pinch salt
1 egg
a little milk

Rub butter into flour. Add remaining dry ingredients. Beat egg into milk, then add to mix to make a stiff dough. Roll out to ½ in/1 cm thick and cut into small rounds. Place on a greased baking sheet and bake in a pre-heated oven, Gas 6/400°F/200°C, for 10 minutes, or until golden brown.

Serves 4

MALT LOAF

An old-time teatime favourite from *Bamber Gascoigne* – delicious spread with unsalted butter. Measure out malt and syrup with a spoon dipped in boiling water.

2 oz/50 g butter
4 oz/100 g golden syrup
4 oz/100 g malt extract
4 tbsp milk
8 oz/200 g self-raising flour
pinch salt
4 oz/100 g sultanas
1 egg, beaten

Grease a 2 lb/900 g loaf tin and line with greased greaseproof paper. Put butter, syrup, malt and milk into a saucepan and heat gently until butter melts. Sift flour and salt together in a bowl. Add sultanas. Stir in warmed butter mixture and egg. Beat until smooth. Pour into tin and bake at Gas 3/325°F/160°C for 1½ hours or until firm to touch. Leave in tin for a few minutes before turning out on to wire tray to cool. Cut into slices and spread with butter to serve. For a really sticky cake, wrap in foil and leave for a few days before eating.

Serves 8

ARSENAL BUNS

Similar to Chelsea buns, these are *Brian Moore*'s sticky fruit favourites.

2 oz/50 g caster sugar
¼ pint/150 ml each, tepid water and milk
1 level tbsp dried yeast
1¼ lb/600 g plain flour
1 tsp salt
2 oz/50 g butter
1 egg, beaten
1 oz/25 g butter, melted
2 oz/50 g soft brown sugar
4 oz/100 g mixed dried fruit
½ tsp cinnamon
1 tbsp honey, melted
2 oz/50 g icing sugar, sifted
a little water
glacé cherries, halved

Stir 1 tsp sugar into water and milk. Stir in yeast and leave until frothy (about 15 minutes). Sieve flour and salt into a bowl. Rub in butter, stir in remaining sugar. Make a well in the centre, add egg and yeast liquid and mix to a dough with a fork. Put in a clean bowl, cover with a damp cloth and leave in a warm place to double in size.

Knock-back dough and roll into a large rectangle on a floured surface. Brush dough with melted butter, sprinkle over sugar, dried fruit and cinnamon. Roll up and cut into 9 equal portions. Place in a greased 8 in/20 cm cake tin and leave to prove for 30 minutes covered with a damp cloth. Brush with honey. Cook at Gas 7/425°F/220°C for 20 minutes or until browned. Leave in tin for 10 minutes before removing to cool on a wire rack.

Mix icing sugar with enough water to make a thin icing to drizzle over the top of the buns. Top with glacé cherries.

Makes 9 buns

SWEET NOTHING

Irresistible fruit-topped cheesecake from actress *Emma Wray*.

8 oz/225 g digestive biscuits, crushed
4 oz/100 g butter, melted
1 sachet gelatine
3 tbsp water
3 eggs, separated
6 oz/150 g caster sugar
8 oz/225 g cream cheese
vanilla essence
½ pint/300 ml double cream, lightly whipped
2 bananas, peeled and sliced on the slant
2 oranges, peeled, sliced and cut into wedges
2 oz/50 g white grapes, halved
1 oz/25 g frozen raspberries, defrosted
4 tbsp apricot jam
2 tbsp water

Mix biscuits into butter. Press into base of a round, greased 8 in/20 cm loose-bottomed cake tin. Leave to set in fridge.

Sprinkle gelatine over water and leave to soak. Beat yolks and sugar together until light and fluffy. Beat in cream cheese and a few drops of vanilla essence. Dissolve gelatine in a bowl over a pan of hot water. Beat into cheese mix. Fold in cream and stiffly beaten egg whites. Pour over biscuit base and set in fridge.

Once set, remove cheesecake from tin and place on serving dish. Arrange fruit on top. Heat jam with water, sieve, cool and brush over fruit.

Serves 6-8

COOKING FOR CHRISTMAS

Most of the traditional Christmas cooking can be done in advance. The pud, the cake, even the mince for pies taste much better with time to mature.
Turkey has become the traditional Christmas feast. But in recent years supermarkets are selling the real old-fashioned taste of Christmas – a goose. The meat is dark and tasty and there are acres of crackly skin. The perfect bird for a once-a-year celebration.

MÉNAGE À TROIS

A traditional Christmas feast from Rebecca Lacey and Rhoda Lewis who starred in ITV's popular series 'The Bretts'.

Boned turkey stuffed with a boned duck stuffed with a boned poussin stuffed with an egg. Ask your butcher to do the boning.

Stuffing
1 onion, peeled and chopped
3 oz/75 g breadcrumbs
salt and pepper
4 oz/100 g chestnut purée
2 oz/50 g flaked almonds
2 tbsp milk
1 egg, hard-boiled and shelled

10 lb/4.5 kg turkey boned (weight before boning)
3 lb/1.4 kg duck, boned
1 lb/450 g poussin, boned

Mix onion, breadcrumbs, salt, pepper, purée, almonds and milk. Wrap mixture around egg and stuff poussin cavity. Sprinkle poussin with salt and pepper. Push poussin into duck cavity. Sprinkle duck with salt and pepper. Push into turkey cavity. Sprinkle top with salt and pepper. Sew up both ends of turkey. Put on roasting rack and cook 20 minutes per 1 lb/450 g plus 20 minutes at Gas 4/ 350°F/180°C until golden brown. The turkey will reform its shape during cooking. To serve, carve across in thick slices.

Serves 12

ROAST GOOSE

Goose has dark meat and makes a festive change from turkey. Defrost thoroughly, as for turkey, cook and serve with forcemeat goosebumps and SAUCE RUDOLPH.

12 lb/4.7 kg oven-ready goose, giblets removed, rinsed and thoroughly dried
salt and pepper

Goosebumps
6 oz/175 g fresh white breadcrumbs
1 small onion, peeled and finely chopped
1 cooking apple, cored and grated
1 tsp fresh sage, chopped
salt and pepper
1 egg, beaten
2 tbsp milk
oil for frying

Pack your favourite stuffing into neck-end of goose. Place goose on a trivet in a roasting tin, prick all over with a fork and bake in a pre-heated oven at Gas 6/400°F/200°C for 30 minutes. Turn oven down to Gas 4/350°F/180°C for 2 hours, or until juices run clear when thigh is pierced with a skewer. Carefully drain fat from roasting tin every 30 minutes or so.

For the goosebumps (ingredients make 12), mix breadcrumbs, onion, apple, sage, salt and pepper in a bowl. Stir in egg and enough milk to bind. Form into small balls and deep-fry in hot oil until brown. Drain. Place round goose with chipolata sausages, bacon rolls and roast potatoes.

Serves 6

SAUCE RUDOLPH

6 tbsp redcurrant jelly
¼ pint/150 ml red wine
rind and juice of 1 orange
1 tsp cornflour mixed to a paste with water
pinch of cinnamon

Place jelly, wine, orange juice and rind in a small pan. Gently heat until jelly melts. Stir in cornflour paste and cinnamon, bring to the boil and simmer for 2-3 minutes. Serve with goose.

Makes ½ pint/300 ml

RUM AND GINGER BUTTER

Delicious rum butter spiked with chopped stem ginger to serve with the pud.

4 oz/100 g unsalted butter, softened
6 oz/175 g icing sugar, sifted
2 oz/50 g stem ginger, chopped
2 tbsp rum

Blend butter with icing sugar. Stir in stem ginger and rum and place in a small pot. Chill and serve with Christmas pudding.

Makes 12 oz/325 g

CHRISTMAS GREENS

1 lb/450 g Brussels sprouts, trimmed
1 lb/450 g broccoli, trimmed and cut into florets
8 oz/225 g green beans, trimmed
8 oz/225 g mangetout, trimmed

Rinse Brussels sprouts, broccoli and beans in clean water and plunge into boiling salted water. Simmer for 5 minutes. Rinse mangetout and add to pan; cook for a further 2 minutes. Drain and arrange on serving plate.

Serves 6

BRANDY SNAPS

4 oz/100 g butter
4 oz/100 g caster sugar
4 oz/100 g golden syrup
4 oz/100 g plain flour, sifted
juice of ½ lemon
pinch ground ginger

Place butter, sugar and syrup in a pan. Gently heat until butter melts and sugar dissolves. Remove from heat. Stir in flour, lemon juice and ginger. Place small teaspoonfuls of mixture, 3 at a time, on to a greased baking sheet, and bake at Gas 5/375°F/ 190°C for approximately 5 minutes or until dark golden brown. Cool slightly, remove with a greased palette knife and quickly wrap around the end of a greased wooden spoon handle.

Makes 36 approx

APRICOT MINCE PIES

Delicate orange-flavoured pastry with a piece of apricot in the base of the tart and mincemeat on top.

8 oz/200 g plain flour, sifted
pinch salt
1 tsp grated orange rind
2 oz/50 g butter
2 oz/50 g lard
4 tbsp water
15 oz/425 g can apricot halves, drained and cut in half
4 tbsp mincemeat
1 egg white, lightly beaten
caster sugar for sprinkling

Sift flour and salt into a bowl. Stir in rind and rub in fats until mixture resembles breadcrumbs. Make a well in the centre, and add water to mix to a dough. Knead lightly, wrap and chill for 30 minutes.

Roll pastry out on a lightly-floured board. Cut circles using fluted pastry cutter. Line greased patty tins with half the pastry circles. Place apricot in the base, top with a little mincemeat. Dampen pastry edges with water and place remaining circles on top. Seal edges. Brush with egg white; sprinkle with caster sugar. Make a tiny hole in centre of each, and bake at Gas 6/400°F/200°C for 10-15 minutes or until pastry is golden brown.

Remove from oven and cool on a wire rack.

Makes 20

On Christmas morning, when we've grumbled at the kids for waking us at 6 a.m., gone back to bed for a snooze and finally emerged, blinking, to shove the turkey in the oven at 8 a.m., it may come as some consolation that the TV-am team has already done a day's work.

Early-rising presenters need to be well fed to keep them alert. The TV-am canteen is renowned for its hard-to-resist, super 'full' breakfast: bacon, sausages, eggs, tomatoes, mushrooms, black pudding and sauté potatoes. But here are the special festive breakfasts, chosen by the TV-am team.

SANTA'S GOGGLES

Lightly-poached eggs on toast spread with gentleman's relish – anchovy paste.

4 eggs
4 buttered toast rounds
1 tbsp Gentleman's relish
salt
parsley and watercress, to garnish

Break eggs into lightly-oiled ramekin dishes. Place in a pan of simmering water, to come halfway up sides of dish. Cook until eggs are just set. Spread toast with a little relish, and place egg on top. Season with a little salt and garnish with parsley and watercress.

Serves 4

ORIENTAR

Thick, rich and creamy Greek yoghurt with chopped apple, pear and banana sprinkled with demerara sugar.

1 pint/600 ml thick Greek yoghurt
1 red-skinned apple, cored and chopped
1 pear, cored and chopped
1 orange, peeled and cut into wedges
1 banana, peeled and sliced
2 tbsp demerara sugar

Mix yoghurt, apple and pear together. Spoon into individual bowls and decorate with orange wedges and banana slices. Sprinkle sugar over banana slices.

Serves 4

FIRST NOËL

Delicious mix of fruit juices for a healthy start to Christmas Day. The truly decadent could add varying proportions of sparkling wine for a festive fizz.

1¾ pint/1 litre orange juice
1¾ pint/1 litre pineapple juice
wineglassful grenadine
fizzy wine or mineral water (optional)
orange and lemon slices, to garnish

Mix all ingredients together and pour into chilled glasses decorated with orange and lemon slices.

Serves 8

FEAST OF STEPHEN

Luxury dish of spicy rice and crisp bacon, smoked salmon and capers, decorated with hard-boiled eggs.

8 oz/225 g long grain rice, rinsed
1 tsp turmeric
4 rashers back bacon, de-rinded
1 tbsp capers
salt and fresh ground black pepper
4 oz/100 g smoked salmon
2 hard-boiled eggs, cut into quarters

Add rice to a large pan of lightly-salted boiling water, stir in turmeric and cook until rice is tender. Drain. Grill bacon until crisp, and snip into chunks. Mix with rice, capers, salt and pepper, and pile on a plate. Cut salmon into thin strips and lay in a criss-cross pattern over rice. Decorate with egg.

Serves 4

DING DONG MERRILY

Half a Galia melon filled with flaked smoked haddock and dressed with lemon juice for a lovely mix of flavours.

2 Galia melons, halved
1 lb/450 g smoked haddock fillet, cooked
1 tbsp lemon juice
ground black pepper
1 lemon, sliced for garnish

Remove seeds from melons and scoop out a little flesh. Skin, bone and flake haddock, sprinkle with lemon juice and season with pepper. Spoon into hollowed melon halves. Serve garnished with a few slices of lemon.

Serves 4

FIGGY

The usual muesli oat-and-flake mix but with Christmas pudding fruits added.

6 oz/175 g rolled oats
6 oz/175 g bran or wheatgerm
2 oz/50 g nuts, chopped
1 oz/25 g dates, chopped
1 oz/25 g dried figs, chopped
1 oz/25 g raisins
1 oz/25 g dried apricots, chopped
½ tsp mixed spice
2 satsumas, peeled and broken into segments
milk to serve

Mix oats, bran, nuts, dates, figs, raisins, apricots and mixed spice in a large bowl. Spoon into serving bowls and decorate with satsuma segments and serve with milk.

Serves 4

High jinx after the show at TV-am's Christmas breakfast party.

MERRY GENTLEMAN

Light omelette filled with sliced button mushrooms.

3 eggs, beaten
3 tsp water
salt and pepper
2 oz/50 g button mushrooms, wiped and sliced
1 oz/25 g butter

Garnish
1 tomato, sliced
1 slice toast, crusts removed, in triangles
watercress

Beat eggs and water and season. Fry mushrooms in butter until lightly browned. When fat is hot, pour in egg mix and swirl round with a fork so the uncooked mixture runs underneath. As soon as the omelette begins to set and while the top is still runny, flip over and tip on a serving plate.

Garnish with tomatoes and toast triangles with watercress.

Serves 1

Cooking for Children

Children love to help in the kitchen and with proper supervision they can make many recipes themselves. Even the youngest can help with stirring and mixing. And there's nothing they love more than licking out the bowl.

Benny Hill's Little Angel's who appear on his show love to help 'Uncle Benny' in the kitchen.

KIDS' KRUNCH

Mixed cereal breakfast for children to make on their own.

2 oz/50 g each Coco Pops, Rice Krispies, Frosties, Honey Smacks, rolled oats
fresh, cold milk
sugar

Mix cereals and divide into bowls. Pour over milk and add sugar before serving.

Serves 4

ROCKETS

Individual trifles packed with fruit and topped with a chocolate flake.

4 oz/100 g frozen raspberries, defrosted
½ pint/300 ml made-up liquid raspberry jelly
14 oz/400 g tin custard
¼ pint/150 ml double cream
1 chocolate flake, cut into 4

Divide raspberries between 4 glasses and pour over jelly to cover. Leave to set in fridge. Pour over a layer of custard. Whip cream until softly thick and pipe a swirl on top. Decorate with chocolate flake.

Serves 4

'FOR UNCLE BENNY' CAKE

Foolproof cake to ice for special occasions.

1 lb/450 g soft margarine
1 lb/450 g caster sugar
8 eggs
1 lb/450 g self-raising flour, sifted
8 tbsp apricot jam
1½ lb/700 g white, ready-to-roll fondant icing
few drops blue colouring
12 oz/350 g icing sugar, sifted
6 oz/175 g butter, softened
few drops pink colouring

Grease and line a 10 in/25 cm square cake tin. Pre-heat oven to Gas 4/350°F/180°C. Cream margarine and sugar until light and fluffy. Beat in eggs thoroughly, two at a time. Carefully fold in flour. Spoon mixture evenly into tin, smooth surface and bake for 1 hour or until springy to touch and golden. Rest in tin for 10 minutes, and turn out on to a cooling rack. Remove paper and cool.

Carefully cut cake in half horizontally and fill with 6 tbsp jam (if necessary, warm jam to make spreading easier). Place cake on board, and brush all over with remaining jam. Colour fondant icing evenly with blue working it in with fingertips. Sprinkle a little cornflour on a work surface, roll out fondant to size of cake. Cover cake and trim. Beat icing sugar into butter. Add pink colouring. Pipe shells around base of cake, and your own message on top.

Serves 20

Benny Hill's Little Angels bake him a cake.

CHEESE-STIX

Easy enough for kids to make, but a good recipe for unskilled grown-ups, too.

7 oz/200 g frozen puff pastry, defrosted
1 egg, beaten
2 oz/50 g Cheddar cheese, grated

Roll out pastry into a rectangle on a lightly floured board. Cut into ½ in/1 cm-wide strips. Brush with egg, twist and place on a greased baking sheet. Sprinkle over cheese and cook at Gas 7/425°F/ 220°C for 6 minutes or until golden. Carefully remove and cool on a wire rack.

Makes 30

BANGER-BURGERS

A cross between a sausage and a burger. It is made with sausagemeat and moulded into flat cakes before frying. An easy dish for kids to make – with supervision for the frying.

1 small onion, peeled and chopped
1 lb/450 g sausagemeat
1 tsp chives, chopped
1 tbsp tomato purée
fresh ground black pepper
flour for coating
4 rolls, halved
4 lettuce leaves and tomato slices, to serve

Mix the onion, sausagemeat, chives, tomato purée and pepper together. Shape into 4 even-sized burgers and coat in flour. Fry in oil for about 5 minutes each side or until golden and crisp on the outside, and cooked through. Serve in rolls with lettuce and tomato.

Serves 4

Savoury Cheese-Stix (see page 107).

Wizard Treats for children's parties conjured up by Mr Majeika, alias *Stanley Baxter*.

ABRACADABRA

Sandwich loaf filled with salmon (use other fillings to taste: such as egg mayonnaise and cress, sardines, grated cheese and pickle) covered with smooth cream cheese and decorated with tiny cut-out hearts, diamonds, clubs and spades. Use shaped cutters for this.

1 unsliced wholemeal loaf
1 oz/25 g butter, softened
15 oz/425 g tin red salmon, drained and mashed
2 tbsp mayonnaise
ground black pepper
1 lb/450 g cream cheese

Decorations
½ red pepper, thinly pared
aubergine skin, parsley to garnish

Remove crusts from bread, and slice into 3 horizontally. Spread slices with butter. Mix salmon with mayonnaise and pepper and make into a three-layer sandwich. Place on serving plate and spread cream cheese all over. Decorate with cut-out shapes from pepper and aubergine skin. Garnish with parsley.

Makes 8 slices

SORCERER'S SCORCHER

Scarlet and delicious home-made tomato soup with witch's hat croûtons on top.

1 onion, peeled and chopped
1 celery stick, washed and chopped
1 small potato, peeled and chopped
3 tbsp oil
2 tbsp tomato purée
1 tsp sugar
2 lb/900 g tomatoes, peeled and chopped
1½ pints/850 ml chicken stock
1 bay leaf
salt and fresh ground black pepper
4 slices bread, cut into witch's hat shapes

Fry onion, celery and potato in oil for 5 minutes. Stir in tomato purée and sugar. Add tomatoes, stock, bay leaf and season with salt and pepper. Bring to the boil and simmer for 25 minutes. Remove bay leaf and liquidise until smooth. Fry hat-shaped croûtons until golden brown; float on top.

Serves 4

MAGIC WANDS

Tasty mince moulded round toffee-apple sticks to make wizard wands. Dip into spicy peanut sauce.

1 lb/450 g minced beef
1 egg, beaten
salt and fresh ground pepper
1 tbsp tomato purée
½ tsp dried thyme

Peanut sauce
4 tbsp crunchy peanut butter
¼ pint/150 ml milk
squirt of lemon juice
large pinch chilli powder

Bind the mince, egg, salt and pepper, tomato purée and dried thyme together and mould on to wooden sticks. Grill gently until browned and cooked through.
    To make the sauce, mix all ingredients together. Pour into a bowl and serve with wands.

Makes 8

Spangles

Star-shaped, puff-pastry savouries filled with smooth pâté.

7 oz/200 g packet frozen puff pastry, defrosted
1 egg, beaten
1 tbsp sesame seeds
4 oz/100 g smooth liver pâté

Roll out pastry on a lightly-floured board. Make star shapes with a cutter. Place on a greased baking sheet and brush with egg. Sprinkle over sesame seeds. Cook at Gas 7/425°F/220°C for 5 minutes. Cool, then split horizontally. Fill with pâté.

Makes 20 stars

Blackcurrant Brew

Pretty, pale-lavender-coloured milky drink, delicious and refreshing served chilled.

¼ pint/150 ml plain yoghurt
¼ pint/150 ml chilled milk
1 oz/25 g blackcurrants, puréed
2 tbsp Ribena, or blackcurrant cordial
few blackcurrants or leaves, to garnish

Place ingredients in a blender until smooth. Pour into a tall glass and decorate with blackcurrants or leaves.

Serves 1

Hocus Pocus

Toast moon and cat shapes covered with chocolate spread and lemon curd.

6 slices bread
chocolate spread
lemon curd
red liquorice and nuts for decoration

Use kitchen scissors to cut out cat and moon shapes from bread slices. Toast each side and spread chocolate over cats and lemon curd over moon. Make cats' faces with nuts and liquorice.

Makes 3 cats and 3 moons

A magic treat for children – Magic Wands.

Gudrun Ure, who is usually beetling about as Supergran, would make all this fun food for her 'grandchildren'.

Crunchy Drumsticks

Skinned chicken drumsticks with a crunchy overcoat of crushed potato crisps.

8 chicken drumsticks
1 egg, beaten
1 packet plain crisps, crushed

Skin and trim drumsticks. Dip in beaten egg. Spread crisps on greaseproof paper, roll drumsticks in crisps and coat well. Place on baking tray and cook at Gas 6/400°F/200°C for 25 minutes, or until cooked through. Garnish with watercress if desired.

Serves 4

Little Women

Slices of bread cut into lady shapes covered with melted cheese.

8 slices bread
4 oz/100 g Cheddar cheese, grated
Marmite for decoration

Using a gingerbread woman cutter, cut out shapes from bread. Toast one side, turn over and cover with grated cheese. Grill until melted. Paint on Marmite eyes and mouth for decoration, using the point of a cocktail stick.

Serves 4

Chequerboard Sandwich

Gudrun Ure, alias 'Supergran' has lots of tea-time treats in store.

Tiny square sandwiches of brown and white bread arranged to look like a chequerboard.

3 oz/75 g butter, softened
12 slices brown bread
9 slices white bread
4 hard-boiled eggs, shelled
4 tbsp mayonnaise
salt and pepper
4 oz/100 g smooth liver pâté
tomato and watercress to garnish

Lightly butter the bread. Mash eggs, mayonnaise, salt and pepper. Use with white bread to make 3 triple-decker sandwiches. Trim crusts to make a neat square, and cut into 4 small squares. Make 4 brown triple-decker sandwiches with liver pâté. Trim as above. Assemble alternate squares of bread to make a chequerboard effect. Garnish with tomato quarters and watercress.

Serves 8

GINGERBREAD COTTAGE

Impressive but easy-to-make cottage cake, using bought cake.

12 oz/350 g icing sugar, sifted
6 oz/175 g soft margarine
few drops pink colouring
3 bought rectangular ginger cakes
1 small packet Shreddies
4 oz/100 g white marzipan, coloured red with few
    drops of colouring
1 oz/25 g white marzipan
2 strips black liquorice
4 oz/100 g desiccated coconut
few drops green colouring
1 oz/25 g green marzipan
few bought icing flowers

Beat icing sugar into margarine until smooth. Add pink colouring and beat until blended. Sandwich 2 ginger cakes together with icing, and place on silver board. Cut remaining cake at an angle to make the roof. Stick on top with icing. Carefully spread remaining icing over cake to cover, and smooth with a knife. Stick on Shreddies to make roof, starting at the bottom. Mould a chimney using 1 oz/25 g red marzipan. Make a hole in the top and stick in a piece of liquorice. Place chimney on top of cake, removing Shreddies if necessary to fit. Roll out more red marzipan and cut out a door shape. Reserve scraps. Make door knocker and hinges out of liquorice and press into marzipan. Stick door on to cake. Roll out white marzipan, and cut into squares to make windows. Cut curtain shapes from red marzipan and press on. Trim with strips of liquorice. Press windows on to cake. Make toadstools with remaining red and white marzipan. Put 3 oz/75 g coconut into a polythene bag. Add a few drops of green colouring and shake well to colour. Spread over silver board for grass, and make a path with the remaining white coconut. Roll green marzipan into small balls, and stick on icing flowers. Stick into green coconut grass, with the marzipan toadstools.

Serves 12

TOFFEE APPLES

Sweet apples covered in crackly toffee. Note: children must only make these with help, as the toffee is very hot.

8 dessert apples
8 wooden sticks
8 oz/225 g granulated sugar
½ pint/300 ml water

Wash and thoroughly dry apples, and push sticks into stem end. Put sugar and water in a large, heavy-based pan, and heat gently until sugar dissolves. Bring to boil, and boil rapidly until it turns brown. Tilt pan and quickly dip each apple in the liquid, rotating them so the toffee coats them completely. Place on oiled greaseproof paper and leave to set.

Serves 8

CHOCOLATE BANANA LOLLIES

Frozen bananas dipped in chocolate and crushed nuts.

4 bananas, peeled and cut in half
8 lolly sticks
8 oz/225 g plain cooking chocolate
1 oz/25 g chopped mixed nuts
1 oz/25 g desiccated coconut
1 potato

Push bananas on to lolly sticks, place on greaseproof paper and freeze overnight. Melt chocolate in a bowl over hot water. Dip bananas into chocolate to coat, using a spoon to cover. Quickly sprinkle nuts or coconut over the coated bananas. Stick into potato to keep upright and leave to set.

Makes 8

PACKED SCHOOL DINNERS

Gian Sammarco, alias Adrian Mole, recalls that the worst thing about his own school was the dinners. And the worst thing about school dinners was the dinner ladies. 'They were huge and terrifying with wrinkled stockings and faces to match. They had names like Mrs Happy and their enormous motherly bosoms, supposedly encasing hearts of gold, temporarily hoodwinked you. But as soon as they opened their mouths to bellow "PEAS???!!???" you were reduced to a quivering wreck.' So with his gastronomic nerves in tatters, Gian turned to packed school lunches.

TAJ MAJAL

Packed lunch based on Indian foods – spicy Tandoori chicken drumsticks, samosas (crackly pastry triangles filled with mildly spiced vegetables), Bombay mix snack, cucumber sticks, plan yoghurt, a banana and Indian sweetmeats.

TANDOORI DRUMSTICKS

4 chicken drumsticks, skinned
salt
lemon juice
2 tsp Tandoori powder
3 tbsp plain yoghurt
ground black pepper

Prick drumsticks all over with a fork. Rub in salt and lemon juice, then leave for an hour. Mix Tandoori powder into yoghurt with pepper. Coat drumsticks with paste and marinate for another hour. Grill for about 8 minutes each side, or until cooked through.

Makes 4

LEMON AND ALMOND BRITTLE

4 oz/100 g sugar
¼ pint/150 ml water
1 tbsp cornflour mixed into 1 tbsp water
1 tsp lemon juice
1 oz/25 g unsalted butter
1 oz/25 g flaked almonds

Dissolve sugar in water over low heat. Bring to boil for 4-5 minutes. Remove from heat. Add cornflour mix and return to heat, stirring until thickened. Add lemon juice, then butter, piece by piece, until absorbed. Stir in flaked almonds, then turn out into a greased shallow tin and smooth over. Mark into squares. Break up when completely cold.

Serves 2

FRUIT AND NUT CASE

Meat-free lunch for vegetarian food enthusiasts, consisting of tartlet quiches made from left-over pastry; a salad; oatjacks (oat bars made with dark brown sugar and sultanas); freshly squeezed orange juice.

OATJACKS

4 oz/100 g margarine
4 oz/100 g soft dark brown sugar
1 level tbsp golden syrup
5 oz/150 g rolled oats
1 oz/25 g sultanas

Melt margarine in a pan with sugar and syrup. Stir in oats and sultanas. Turn into a greased 1 lb/450 g loaf tin. Flatten. Bake at Gas 4/350°F/180°C for 25 minutes until brown. Cut into bars when cold.

Makes 8

TUCK BOX

The great British packed lunch with tomato soup in a flask, a banger-filled roll and a pear stuffed with Cheddar.

TOMATO SOUP

1 stick celery, chopped
1 small onion, peeled and chopped
1 carrot, peeled and chopped
2 rashers bacon, de-rinded and chopped
1 oz/25 g butter
2 tbsp plain flour
1 tbsp tomato purée
1 lb/450 g tomatoes, skinned and chopped
1½ pts/900 ml chicken stock
salt and white pepper
bouquet garni

Gently fry celery, onion, carrot and bacon in butter for 5 minutes, until soft. Stir in flour and tomato purée. Add tomatoes, stock, seasoning and bouquet garni. Bring to boil, cover and simmer gently for about 30 minutes. Remove bouquet garni and liquidise soup. Return to clean pan, heat through and adjust seasoning.

Serves 4

BABY QUICHE WITH ONION AND TOMATO

4 oz/100 g shortcrust pastry (or left-over pastry)
1 small onion, peeled and thinly sliced
½ oz/15 g butter
1 tomato, de-seeded and chopped
1 egg
¼ pint/150 ml milk
salt and pepper

Roll out pastry and cut out 12 rounds. Grease a patty tin and fill with pastry. Place for 15 minutes in fridge. Gently fry onion in butter until soft. Remove from heat and stir in tomato. Divide between pastry cases. Beat egg, milk and seasoning together in a jug. Fill cases. Bake at Gas 6/400°F/200°C for 10-15 minutes until golden. Cool on wire rack.

Makes 12

CHEESE IN A PEAR

4 pears
4 oz/100 g Cheddar cheese

Using a corer, remove cores from centre of pears.
Still using corer, cut cylinders out of block of
cheese. Insert cheese in hole in pears where cores
were.

Makes 4

HAVE A NICE DAY

Yankee doodle dandy lunchbox with a BLT
(bacon, lettuce and tomato double decker
sandwich), tub of coleslaw, popcorn, cola and, of
course, a big apple.

BLT

3 slices wholemeal bread, buttered
2 tsp mayonnaise
4 rashers bacon, fried crisp
2 leaves Iceberg lettuce
1 medium tomato, sliced

Spread mayonnaise on lightly buttered bread.
Then divide bacon, lettuce and tomato slices
between two slices. Pile up, then top with
remaining slice for a double decker.

Makes 1 sandwich

COLESLAW

4 oz/100 g white cabbage, finely shredded
2 carrots, peeled and grated
2 tbsp soured cream
squeeze of lemon juice
dash of paprika
salt and pepper

Mix all ingredients and pack into an empty, clean
margarine tub with a lid.

Serves 2

PACKED-A-LUNCHA

A lunch with an Italian flavour. Super pasta salad
with Mortadella sausage or tuna and red peppers, a
beefsteak tomato, bread sticks and bunch of
grapes.

PASTA MORTADELLA

4 oz/100 g cooked pasta shells
¼ red pepper, de-seeded and thinly sliced
1 oz/25 g cooked green beans
2 oz/50 g Mortadella sausage, in strips, or 2oz/50g
   tuna, drained and flaked
1 tbsp mayonnaise
salt and pepper

Mix all ingredients and pack into an empty, clean
margarine tub with a lid.

Serves 1

Drinks

Long hot summer days and evenings are the perfect occasion for refreshing drinks made from fresh fruits or vegetables. Sometimes, however, a colourful alcoholic cocktail will fit the bill. Included here are a selection of all star tipples – plus a couple of stimulating pick-me-ups. Before pouring your chosen drink frost the glass by dipping the rim in juice then into caster sugar. Use fresh fruit slices as a pretty decoration.

FIZZY LIZZY

A refreshing green mint drink (pictured opposite) made from the products of *Jill Gascoine*'s herb garden.

4 tbsp mint, chopped
1 tsp sugar
¼ pint/150 ml boiling water
juice of ½ lemon
½ pint/300 ml ginger ale
1 egg white, lightly whisked
1 tbsp caster sugar
crushed ice
mint leaves and 4 cocktail cherries to decorate

Put mint and sugar in a heatproof jug. Pour over boiling water. Leave to cool. Add lemon juice and strain through a sieve into a clean jug. Top with ginger ale. Dip rims of cocktail glasses into egg white, and then caster sugar to coat. Put crushed ice into glasses, and pour over mint cocktail. Decorate with mint leaves and cherries.

Serves 4

BLUE MONK

You've heard of pink champagne. Here's blue champagne! It's coloured with a dash of blue curaçao, an orange-flavoured liqueur. Use the palest champagne or dry sparkling wine, or even lemonade for a much less alcoholic version. A delicious drink enjoyed by prankster *Jeremy Beadle*.

1 bottle pale champagne, sparkling wine or lemonade
2 tbsp blue curaçao

Pour champagne into a glass jug. Add blue curaçao and stir. Pour into glasses.

Makes 6 glasses

Two fast pick-me ups for early morning risers like the staff at TV-am.

PRAIRIE OYSTER

This is an age-old hangover cure. You have to close your eyes and gulp it down in one go without breaking the egg yolk. Do this and survive, and you deserve to be cured!

1 egg yolk
1 tsp Worcestershire sauce
dash of vinegar
salt and pepper

Tip egg yolk into a glass and pour over sauce, vinegar and seasoning. Drink.

VIRGIN MARY

Reviving cocktail of juice and Worcestershire sauce.

1 pint/600 ml tomato juice
4 tsp Worcestershire sauce, or to taste

Pour juice into tall-stemmed glasses. Add Worcestershire sauce to taste before serving.

Serves 4

Bob Holness, host of ITV's popular quiz show, 'Blockbusters', is a wine enthusiast who can knock up a mean cocktail when the occasion demands it. Here are 3 alcoholic drinks, plus 2 alcohol-free drinks for children, drivers and those who simply don't drink.

GROWN-UPS' COCKTAILS

MARTINI MARY ROSE

Blush-coloured, delicately-scented martini. But beware. Only drink one, or dilute to taste with soda.

few drops angostura bitters
1 measure gin
2 measures vermouth
slice lemon and orange
green olives

Sprinkle angostura bitters in a cocktail glass, swish round glass and pour away excess. Add gin, vermouth and decorate glass with orange and lemon slices and olives on a cocktail stick.

Ace bartender Bob Holness fixes the drinks.

LEAPFROG

Brilliant green and clear, this drink has a delightful taste of melons with oomph from the rum.

1 measure of Midori melon liqueur
caster sugar
1 measure Bacardi rum
tonic water
squeeze of lime
green glacé cherry to decorate

Dip rim of glass into a little Midori, then into sugar for a frosty sugared rim. Pour in Midori and rum, top up with tonic water and lime juice. Decorate with cherry.

BLUE MOON

Dainty, adult, orange-flavoured blue drink (strange, but true) spiked with vodka and diluted to taste with soda water.

1 measure of blue curaçao
1 measure of vodka
soda water
ice cubes

Pour curaçao and vodka into a stemmed glass. Top up with soda and ice cubes and serve with a blue cocktail stirrer.

KID'S COCKTAILS

BLOCKBUSTER

Delicious fruity cocktail shading from red at the bottom to orange at the top, decorated with blocks of fruit and a cocktail cherry.

fresh chilled orange juice
fresh chilled pineapple juice
lemonade
2 tbsp grenadine
slice of pineapple, orange and a cocktail cherry and
    umbrella to decorate

Pour equal measures of orange juice, pineapple and lemonade into a big glass. Carefully pour in grenadine and decorate.

Serves 1

HOTSPOT

Vivid, clear, red cocktail with a touch of spicy heat from the ginger ale. Decorate with a slice of red-skinned apple for a non-alcoholic, but none-the-less sophisticated, belter of a drink.

1 tbsp concentrated blackcurrant juice
cherryade
ginger ale
red-skinned apple slices for decoration
1 cocktail umbrella

Spoon blackcurrant juice into a stemmed glass. Top up with equal quantities of cherryade and ginger ale. Decorate with apple and umbrella.

Serves 1

GOLD RUN

Sensuous and creamy, frothy, pale gold drink with delicate fruitiness and stylish elegance from the grated chocolate topping.

1 banana, peeled
4 tbsp single cream
lemonade
crushed ice
grated chocolate

Whizz banana and cream in a blender until smooth. Pour into glass and top with chilled lemonade and crushed ice. Sprinkle chocolate over and serve with a straw.

Serves 1

BARRYMORE'S BOUNTY

'I remember the first dish I ever cooked,' says *Michael Barrymore*. 'It was roast chicken and the oven was a hole in the ground. I was 12, in the Boy Scouts and instructed to prepare a meal for the priest, Father Salmon. I dug the hole, lit a fire at the bottom, made a rack of twigs, then kept my fingers crossed and my eyes closed. When I managed to prise it out of the hole, it was perfect!' This was clearly the first tentative step to becoming the super-cook he now is. Together with wife Cheryl, he has collected recipes over the years which have been published.

FISHY BUSINESS

Beautiful pastel-striped fish terrine, wrapped in smoked salmon slices for a real indulgence. But it's just as good without.

1½ lbs/700 g lemon soles
little butter
1 pint/600 ml double cream
4 tbsp tartare sauce,
1½ sachets gelatine
3 tbsp hot water
2 tomatoes, blanched and pulped
½ lb/225 g smoked salmon slices, optional
1 bunch watercress
parsley
lemon slices
fresh snipped chives

Dot sole with butter and lightly grill until just cooked. Skin, bone and flake. Liquidise flesh with cream and tartare sauce. Melt gelatine in water over a pan of simmering water. Add to fish mix. Leave until on the point of setting. Divide into 3. Put one third into an oiled mould or loaf tin lined with clingfilm, and leave to set. Add pulped tomato and 2 oz/50 g chopped smoked salmon, if used, to the second third. Pour over set first layer and leave to set. Finely chop watercress and add to third portion of fish mix. Pour over other two set layers. Leave overnight to chill and set.

Unmould and cover with remaining smoked salmon slices. Decorate with lemon slices and chopped chives.

Serves 6

LIME COOLER

juice of 3 oranges
juice of 2 lemons
lime juice cordial
water to taste
1 orange, sliced
1 lemon, sliced
parsley sprigs
lemon peel twist

Pour juices and cordial in a glass jug. Add water to taste. Float orange and lemon slices in layers at the top of the jug. Decorate with parsley and lemon peel twist.

MICHAEL'S GRAPE MOUNTAIN

Black grapes stuffed with cheese for nibbles with drinks.

6 oz/150 g German Brie with green peppercorns, softened
3 oz/75 g cream cheese, softened
1 large bunch black grapes
1 small bunch seedless green grapes

Gently mash Brie and cream cheese, taking care not to crush peppercorns. Chill. Cut grapes almost in half, and remove seeds. Stuff with cheese mix. Pile on a serving plate and dot with seedless green grapes to make a mountain.

PARSNIP CHIPS

These may look like chips, but they taste completely different.

2 tbsp oil
1lb/450 g parsnips peeled and cut into stickes like chips
1½ tbsp tarragon vinegar
1 tsp tandoori spice

Heat oil and sauté chips until just cooked. Add tarragon vinegar and tandoori spice to pan and quickly toss around.

Serves 6

NEW POTATO SALAD

Cold cooked baby potatoes in fresh mayonnaise.

1½ lb/700 g new potatoes, scrubbed, cooked and cooled
½ pint/300 ml mayonnaise, preferably home-made
1 medium onion, peeled and very finely chopped
1 tbsp fresh chopped parsley

Halve potatoes. Mix with mayonnaise and onion. Sprinkle parsley over.

Serves 6

SPICED FILLET OF BEEF

Spiced fillet is a special occasion extravagance. But this recipe works as well with topside if you cook it longer and slower, done to your own preference.

3 lb/1.5 kg fillet of beef, trimmed and tied
3 tbsp olive oil
1 tsp garam masala
2 tsp ground black pepper

Seal beef in hot oil, until browned all over. Sprinkle with garam masala and black pepper. Pre-heat oven to Gas 7/425°F/210°C and cook for 30 minutes. Cool completely.

Serves 6

TOMATO AND CUCUMBER SALAD

Colourful and crunchy salad.

1 lb/450 g hard tomatoes, quartered
1 cucumber, in small chunks
1 bunch spring onions, finely chopped
fresh chopped parsley

Salad dressing
1 tsp Dijon mustard
1 tbsp white wine vinegar
4 tbsp olive oil
salt and fresh ground black pepper

Heap tomatoes, cucumber and onions in a salad bowl. Shake dressing ingredients in a screw-top jar. Pour over salad, toss well, then sprinkle with parsley.

Serves 6

BOMBE BARRYMORE

One of those sensational puddings which are so simple to make. A thin crackly chocolate shell encases a silky and sensuous frozen coffee mousse.

8 oz/225 g plain cooking chocolate
2 tbsp instant coffee
2 tbsp hot water
2 egg whites
4 oz/100 g caster sugar
½ pint/300 ml double cream

Put a 1½ pint/850 ml pudding bowl in the freezer. Melt chocolate in a bowl over a pan of simmering water. Brush inside of chilled bowl with chocolate, painting on more layers as chocolate hardens. Dissolve coffee in water. Whisk egg white stiff, then fold in sugar. Whisk cream thick. Fold coffee into cream, then fold in egg-white mix. Pour filling into set chocolate-lined bowl. Freeze. It unmoulds easily with a gentle shake.

Serves 6

CHERRY MARTINI

An alcoholic cocktail with cherry-filled ice cubes.

cocktail cherries
dry white Martini
lemonade
orange or lemon slices

Place cocktail cherries in ice cube trays. Fill with water and freeze. Mix up equal quantities of Martini and lemonade, or to taste, in a glass jug. Decorate with slices of orange or lemon. Add cherry ice cubes.

FONDUE FEAST

Canadian born disc-jockey *David Jensen* has an international family. Gudrun, his wife, is from Iceland. Daughter Anna Lisa was born in Wimbledon and Alexander in Atlanta, Georgia. With all these world-wide connections it's not surprising that David has a varied taste in food. 'I love anything spicy or exotic. If it's exciting, I'll try it!' Though they eat out quite often, the family most enjoys Gudrun's home cooking. One of the best ways to entertain friends is a fondue party, Gudrun thinks. This way, everyone lends a hand in the preparations, cooking and, of course, the eating.

FISCHLING

Salmon dip with a rough texture. Serve with green crudités.

15 oz/425 g fresh cooked or tinned salmon, drained
12 oz/350 g cream cheese
juice of lemon
dash of tabasco
1 tsp capers
ground black pepper
1 bunch spring onions, trimmed
1 cucumber, cut into sticks
4 sticks celery, cut into strips
1 green pepper, de-seeded and cut into strips

Remove skin and bones from salmon. Blend fish, cream cheese, lemon juice, tabasco, capers and pepper, until smooth. Spoon into serving dish and chill. Serve with vegetable crudités.

Serves 4

LACEY SNAPS

Dainty rolled biscuits for dipping in chocolate fondue (recipe on page 122).

4 oz/100 g butter
4 oz/100 g caster sugar
4 oz/100 g golden syrup
4 oz/100 g plain flour, sifted
juice of ½ lemon
½ tsp ground ginger
½ tsp ground cinnamon

Place butter, sugar and syrup in a pan and gently heat until butter has melted. Stir in flour, lemon juice and spices. Leave to cool. Place teaspoons of mixture on greased baking sheets leaving plenty of room – they spread! Bake at Gas 5/375°F/190°C for 5-7 minutes, until golden and bubbling. Cool slightly, so biscuits are still malleable. Remove from baking sheet with a greased slice and roll round the handle of a wooden spoon. Cool.

Makes 24

STRINGALONG

Scrummy hot cheese dip.

2 cloves garlic, crushed
½ pint/300 ml dry white wine
8 oz/225 g Gruyère cheese
8 oz/225 g Emmental cheese
1 tbsp cornflour
2 tbsp kirsch
freshly ground black pepper

Rub garlic around fondue pan. Pour in wine and gently warm. Gradually add cheese in small lumps, and stir vigorously until melted. Mix cornflour with kirsch to make a thin paste. Add to pan with pepper. Beat well with a wooden spoon until mixture has thickened slightly and is smooth. Keep sauce warm.

Serves 4

The Jensen's enjoying an outdoor Sunday lunch.

ARRAN SALAD

Chunky salad of cauliflower, peppers and spring onions with pine nuts and banana chips.

1 cauliflower, broken into florets and rinsed
1 bunch spring onions, trimmed and chopped
1 red pepper, de-seeded and cut into strips
1 oz/25 g sultanas
2 oz/50 g pine kernels
1 oz/25 g dried banana chips
1 tbsp vinegar
½ tsp mustard
3 tbsp olive oil
1 clove garlic, crushed
salt and pepper

Mix cauliflower, spring onions, pepper, sultanas, pine kernels and banana chips together and arrange in serving dish. Beat vinegar, mustard, oil, garlic and season with salt and pepper, and pour over salad.

Serves 4

BROWN VELVET

Shiny, smooth chocolate dip. Dunk with fruit and home-made biscuits.

3 × 7oz/200 g bars plain chocolate, broken into pieces
½ pint/300 ml water
3 oz/75 g cocoa powder
1 oz/25 g caster sugar

Place all ingredients in a pan. Heat gently until chocolate has melted, and stir until blended. Cool slightly before dipping in seasonal fruit.

Serves 4

ANGEL'S SANDALS

Delicate, airy flat biscuits – super for dipping.

3 large eggs, separated
pinch cream of tartar
4 oz/100 g icing sugar, sifted
½ tsp vanilla essence
2½ oz/65 g plain flour
caster sugar for sprinkling

Beat egg whites with cream of tartar until stiff. Add icing sugar and beat for 1 minute. Fold in egg yolks and essence using a spatula. Sift flour over mixture and fold in. Grease 2 baking sheets and dust with a little flour. Spoon mixture into a large piping bag fitted with a plain nozzle. Pipe 4 in/10 cm by 1 in/2 cm strips of mixture on to baking sheets. Sprinkle heavily with sugar, leave 5 minutes and sprinkle again. Quickly turn baking sheet over and tap with knife to remove excess sugar – the biscuits will stay put! Bake at Gas 3/ 325°F/160°C for 12-15 minutes until straw coloured. Cool and remove from tray. Store in an airtight tin.

Makes 20

LEFT-OVERS

Although he's quite particular about his food, *Ted Rogers* says his wife Marion is such a terrific cook, not much ends up with Dusty Bin! However, there are all too many occasions when we make too much rice or pasta, there's a wedge of cake left-over which nobody seems to want, half a stale loaf stares reproachfully out of the bread bin, and there's the end of the roast to use up and the family are fed-up with Shepherd's Pie yet again. Here are a clutch of ideas for coping with left-overs.

SALAMAGUNDY

A way with left-overs Elizabethan-style. Originally called Solomon Grundy (no one knows why), then Salad MaGundy, it ended up as Salamagundy.

½ Iceberg lettuce, shredded
1 bunch watercress
2 chicken fillets, cooked and in strips
1 can anchovies, drained
4 oz/100 g green beans, cooked
4 hard-boiled eggs, peeled and quartered
2 oz/50 g stoned raisins
6 oz/150 g white grapes, halved and seeded
2 oz/50 g almonds
8 spring onions, trimmed

Dressing
1 tbsp white wine vinegar
4 tbsp olive oil
1 tbsp fresh chopped herbs
salt and fresh ground black pepper

Make a bed of lettuce and watercress on an oval serving platter. Arrange other ingredients in attractive groups on top. Shake dressing ingredients together in a screw-top jar. Pour over salad just before serving and toss well. In summer decorate with marigold or nasturtium petals.

Serves 4

LOAF AND FISH

Savoury bread-and-butter pudding for the days when all there is in the larder is some stale bread, hard cheese, squidgy tomatoes and the remains of a tin of tuna fish.

6 slices of bread, buttered, crusts removed
3 tomatoes, skinned and sliced
4 oz/100 g Cheddar cheese, grated
left-over tuna, drained
1 tbsp capers, chopped
salt and pepper
2 eggs
½ pint/300 ml milk
parsley to garnish

Cut bread into triangles and line base of a buttered ovenproof dish. Put a layer of tomato over and sprinkle with 1 oz/25 g cheese. Mash tuna, capers, salt and pepper together, and put half over cheese. Put another layer of bread on top, then remaining tomatoes and 1 oz/25 g cheese, plus tuna mix. Arrange triangles of bread over top and sprinkle over remaining 2 oz/50 g cheese. Beat together eggs and milk, season with salt and pepper, and pour over pudding. Bake in oven at Gas 5/375°F/190°C, for 30-40 minutes or until bread turns golden. Garnish with parsley sprig.

Serves 4

SPUDDIES

Delicious savoury pancakes – worth cooking too many potatoes for! Flavoured with onions, garlic and parsley, they will also make a very tasty vegetarian main course.

2 lb/900 g potatoes, peeled and boiled
1 small onion, peeled and finely chopped
1 clove garlic, crushed
1 tbsp oil
1 egg, beaten
1 tbsp flour
2 tbsp milk
1 tbsp parsley, chopped
salt and fresh ground black pepper

Mash potatoes in a large bowl. Fry onion and garlic in oil for 3 minutes and remove with a slotted spoon. Add to potatoes, with egg, flour, milk and parsley. Season with salt and pepper, and mix until smooth. Shape mix into pancakes. Adding a little more oil to the pan if necessary, fry pancakes both sides until browned.

Serves 4

TOPNOTCH

The last slice of a cake makes a super crumble topping for left-over tinned fruit.

15 oz/425 g tinned gooseberries, drained
1tsp lemon juice
3 oz/75 g demerara sugar
4 oz/100 g left-over cake

Blend gooseberries with lemon juice and 1 oz/25 g sugar until smooth, and spoon mixture into ramekin dishes. Crumble the cake and mix with rest of demerara sugar. Sprinkle over gooseberries and place under a hot grill until golden. Chill and serve with cream.

Serves 4

EGG-SIT

Way-out omelette filled with croûtons, made from stale bread, and a chopped slice of ham.

12 slices left-over bread, cut into cubes
1 tbsp oil
4 eggs, beaten
2 tsp water
left-over ham, cut into cubes

Fry bread cubes in oil until golden brown. Beat eggs with water and swirl mixture in a hot frying pan until set. Tip croûtons and ham on to omelette, flip over and slide on to a warmed serving plate.

Serves 2

MONDAY SALAD

Substantial salad made from left-over meat and plain boiled vegetables from Sunday lunch. Serve thinly sliced and sparked up with an orange French dressing. Any meat will do, from rare roast beef to chicken.

8 oz/225 g left-over meat, cut into strips
cooked cauliflower, in florets
cooked courgettes, cut into strips
cooked carrots, thinly sliced lengthways

Dressing
4 tbsp oil
1 tbsp orange juice
1 tbsp lemon juice
2 tsp Dijon mustard
1 tsp fresh chives, chopped

Place prepared meat and vegetables in a large serving dish. Shake dressing ingredients in a screw-top jar with chives and pour over the salad.

Serves 4

SHELLEY

If you tend to make too much pasta – and who doesn't – it's the perfect base for a store-cupboard salad. Most fridges have half a pepper and the odd spring onion lying in the salad drawer. And everybody keeps a tin of tuna handy, don't they?

8 oz/225 g pasta shells, cooked
½ red pepper, ½ green pepper, seeded and chopped
7 oz/200 g tin tuna in brine, drained and flaked
2 spring onions, peeled and chopped
6 tbsp mayonnaise
3 tbsp soured cream
1 tbsp lemon juice
salt and ground black pepper

Put pasta, red and green peppers, tuna and onions into a large bowl. Mix mayonnaise with soured cream and lemon juice and stir into the pasta. Season with salt and pepper.

Serves 4

KRAZY KREAM

Stale biscuits soaked in the dregs of a bottle of sherry, stirred into whipped cream, and topped with the last nectarine (or anything else) in the fruit bowl. Mmmm . . . !

6 oz/175 g chocolate digestive biscuits, crushed
2 tbsp sherry
1 pint/600 ml double cream, whipped
1 nectarine, or whatever fruit is available

Place biscuits in a large bowl. Sprinkle over sherry. Fold in ¾ pint/425 ml cream, whipped thoroughly. Divide between 4 tall glasses. Pipe rosettes of remaining cream on top of each one and decorate with fruit slices.

Serves 4

MIRACLE PUDDING

The best way to use up stale cake. Mix into custard and top with meringue.

½ pint/300 ml milk
1 oz/25 g butter
grated rind of 1 lemon
3 oz/75 g cake crumbs
1 oz/25 g caster sugar
2 eggs
2 tbsp raspberry jam
4 oz/100 g caster sugar

Put milk, butter and lemon rind in a saucepan. Bring to boil, then remove from heat. Mix cake crumbs and 1 oz/25 g sugar in a bowl and pour over hot milk. Allow to stand for 30 minutes, stirring occasionally. Separate eggs. Beat in egg yolks. Pour into ovenproof dish. Bake in oven at Gas 4/350°F/180°C, for 45 minutes. Allow to cool and set. Warm jam and spread over. Whisk egg whites until stiff. Add half sugar and continue beating. Add remaining sugar until meringue stands in peaks. Spoon over jam, then fluff up with a fork. Bake at Gas 6/400°F/200°C, for 20 minutes or until golden brown.

Serves 4

INDEX

127

Nata grazie
01463 - 790626.

Nata grazie
01463 - 790626.